DEDICATION

TO THE CHURCH OF ELEVEN22.
I AM SO HONORED TO BELONG TO THIS CHURCH
AND I HOPE THIS ENCOURAGES YOU IN SOME WAY.
THANK YOU FOR BEING WHAT I CONSIDER TO BE
THE BEST CHURCH IN THE WORLD.

A BRIEF WORD

At different times on my 25-year journey as a follower of Jesus,
I have struggled through bible study and personal times in
God's Word. I know it's probably not what you want to hear
when beginning a 40-day devotional written by me, but it's true.
Don't mishear me though, I trust His Word fully, I love it dearly,
and I know it holds the only truth which has the power to set
me free. The problem was I always approached it with a hint of
legalism. A sense of dutiful obligation was the filter by which
I read God's Word, and it often left my devotion time fruitless
and even joyless. Subconsciously I believed the more you read
the more meaningful it would be or that each text needed to be
approached with the purpose of teaching it to someone else.
I am all for long periods of study because there is much to be
gleaned from that kind of effort. I am also a big fan of studying
to teach God's Word to others. Yet I approached God's words
with unnecessary filters which had become a wet blanket over
my intimacy with God through His word. I realize now I had
always been committed to God's Word, but I often missed the
essence of God through His Word.

Then one Christmas I was given 4 or 5 daily devotional studies
by different people. At first, I was kind of like, "Cool, thanks so
much???" kind of like you'd be if you received a fruitcake or
something. They are okay, but they typically sit on the counter
for days on end while everyone overlooks them for the tin of
Christmas cookies. These books were just going to be lumped
on my bookshelf like the other devotionals in which I failed to
find value and meaning. I was just planning to re-gift them to
someone else who may be into those kinds of things. Truthfully,
I dismissed them because they were too short to provide a lot of
meaning and what I believed to be shallow.

It turns out I was wrong, which is usually the case in my life.
About two weeks later I was sitting in my living room waiting
on my family to go somewhere and I just haphazardly picked
up one of the devotionals written by Dr. David Jeremiah and
started reading it. I read it for 3 minutes and thought about it
for 3 hours. The next day, I read the next entry and found myself
repenting of unconfessed sin to the Lord. The following day I

sat silently for a couple of minutes in prayer before reading. Day after day, I found myself picking up that book to spend time with God again. After a couple of months of reading these short and not-so-shallow devotionals, I really began to fall in love with each and every verse of scripture I was studying all over again.

Right in the middle of this season of fresh wind in my life from God's word, my mother-in-law brought me a devotional written by none other than the prince of preachers himself, Charles Spurgeon. It is called Morning and Evening and it is more than wonderful. Each days' writing is short, maybe 300-400 words, but it is incredibly meaningful. Every day my heart was quickened by the Holy Spirit and my love for Jesus was stirred inside me.

This devotional is written in what I hope is the same spirit as the ones that have been such a blessing to me over the last few years. Through these personal times with the Lord, I am able to receive a much-needed kingdom perspective in my life and leadership. I don't know about you, but I need help in daily seeking first His kingdom and righteousness. My hope and prayer is that your study through Jude with me will be exactly that, helpful and encouraging in your pursuit to put the Lord first in all things.

The book of Jude has always been a fascinating letter to me. I believe so many of Jude's warnings and encouragements are just as timely to Jesus' Church today as they have been at any point in our history. I hope each day you are quickened by God's spirit and your love for Jesus is stirred inside you as you study God's words through Jude with me. I genuinely pray your love for God's Word will grow over the next 40 days and you'll learn or be reminded every word in His book matters and has power. Thanks for letting me be a small part of your journey.

Blessings,

COMMENTARY

The book of Jude is titled for its author, Jude, who most scholars agree was the half-brother of Jesus Christ of Nazareth. He identifies himself as the brother of James (1:1) meaning he was probably not the apostle of the same name. His alignment with James is a strong confirmation that he is part of the family of Jesus. Matthew records, "Where did this man get this wisdom and these mighty works? Is not this the carpenter's son? Is not his mother called Mary? And are not his brothers James and Joseph and Simon and Judas?" (Matthew 13:55, emphasis mine). Judas, when translated to English, is often translated as Jude.

The book of 2 Peter shares a lot of similarities to Jude. (I hope to write a 40-day devotional through 2 Peter one day as well!) These similarities in content lead us to believe the date at which they were written are also similar, probably between AD 63 and AD 80. This letter, while short, packs a punch. Jude seems to be a man of few words but when He speaks or writes in this case, it would be wise to listen.

He is a church leader at a time when the Church was full of false teachers, religious extortion, and theological wolves who were preying on God's beloved sheep. Jude was having none of it. It seems his desire and calling were to expose falsehood and sin. He exposed false teachers, faulty thinking, and sin, all while making known the truth to God's church. This letter stands the test of time as it exposes us to the truth of the resurrection, which is the cornerstone of our faith. It also challenges us to examine the way we live and practice our faith so we can contend for the beauty of the Gospel of Jesus Christ in a world that wants us to reject this very message. Jude is a timely invitation if we have ears to hear and it is timely instruction for those of us who want to receive it. [1]

[1] Chuck Swindoll, "Jude," *Insight for Living Ministries,* accessed March 2, 2022, https://insight.org/resources/bible/the-general-epistles/jude.

v. 1 - Jude, a servant of Jesus Christ and brother of James,

What would it be like to be Jesus' brother? What would it take for you to call yourself a servant of your brother? I love my brother but to identify myself as his servant would be a bit of a stretch for me. Most scholars agree Jude and James are included in the 'brothers' who wanted Jesus to go public with His power before it was His time (John 7:1-24). If this is true, as I am apt to believe it to be so, they are also on eternal record as not believing He was actually the Son of God because He wouldn't perform the miracles they expected. To be skeptical of your brother claiming to be God is understandable, that is unless He actually is God which happened to be the case with Jesus.

Some may briefly wonder how they went from this state of unbelief to becoming missionaries carrying the message of Jesus across the known world and writing letters that would encourage believers for millennia to come. If that question crosses your mind too, then you only need to be reminded of one truth, "He is not here, for he has risen, as He said" (Matthew 28:6). [2]

Jude and James' brother was dead, brutally murdered, and then He wasn't dead anymore. He was alive. The resurrection of Jesus from the dead is the reason Jude and James joyfully submitted themselves under Jesus' authority and to His cause. It is the same reason I do and I hope the same reason you do. We do not follow Jesus because of what He will do but because of what He has already done. Be reminded today, believer, Jesus the Christ, the only begotten son of God, put on skin and became sin to endure its curse unto death only to defeat it and come back to life so that by placing our trust in Him we can forever be His brother.

I ask, "What would it be like to be Jesus' brother?" If you have trusted Him as Lord then why don't you tell me, because you, too, are His brother?

---

[2] All Scripture is taken from the English Standard Version unless otherwise noted.

"For those whom he foreknew, he also predestined to be conformed to the image of his Son, in order that he might be the firstborn among many brothers." — *Romans 8:29*

Jesus is your superior older brother. That is a worship-stirring, affection-creating truth for me and I hope it is for you as well. We are so bound to Him and in Him because of what He has done for us that He rejoices in calling us 'brother.' Jesus is glad to have you as His brother or sister. He is not ashamed of you. He is not indignant with you nor will he ever be. He loves you. Rest in that today.

REFLECTION:

What is it like to think of yourself as a brother/sister of Jesus?

How does knowing you are a sibling of Jesus impact your approach to your relationship with Him?

v. 1b - to those who are called, beloved in God the Father and kept for Christ Jesus

I love how Jude addresses his letter to "those who are called, beloved in God…" How do you know if you are among the "called" he is referring to here? Being called is an often-abused term in the Church implying that only some have a connection to God. This just isn't true. We all have a calling and that calling is to be loved by God. You are called to have God's love lavished on you, poured out on your head like Samuel poured the king's oil on the head of David (1 Samuel 16:13). You are called to be overcome with the unrelenting love of God. That is your highest calling.

My counselor once asked me, "How well do you give and receive love?" I had a hard time answering. I found myself breaking people down into categories in my mind who were qualified based on how I thought I treated them. I began to reach for things that gave merit to my lovingness and quickly found my definition of giving love was very transactional and shallow. For me, the measure of how loving I was or how loving someone was toward me was measured based on what we could or were doing for each other. If you needed me and I needed you then we loved each other. As I said, these were very shallow qualifications.

Over the years, I've put together a new definition of love. "Love is when your affections, attention, and desire are purposed on another person and their ultimate good." When I think about loving through that lens, it is easy to see there is a lot of room for growth in my ability to give love; but what really shocked me about the question and my reflection on it was my inability to receive love. I found that I carried - and probably still carry - a tint of distrust toward people which prevents me from really being able to enjoy being loved by them. What a discovery that was for me! I want to live from the place where I trust fully and wholly that I am loved by Him through Jesus Christ and accepted completely based on His merits. I know that all joy and happiness in God comes through receiving the free gift of His love over and over again as He liberally gives it without end. And I want this love to be the source from which all my living and loving is done.

How about you? How well do you give and receive love? We can't really give love until we learn how to receive love. Do you consider yourself to be one of God's beloved children? Do you believe it gives God joy to love you and his love steadfastly holds you in the grip of his grace through Christ Jesus which resounds his glory through eternity? I hope so because it is and it does.

Notice Jude writes we are "...kept for Christ Jesus." Here is how you can rest assured of God's endless love being set on you: it's not for you. It is on you but it is not for you, it is for Jesus. This simply means all the love the Father has for the Son has been placed on you for the sake of Himself. You are kept for His sake which means He will never let go of you because God's character is unchanging and He will always be true to Himself - which means He will always be true to you because He is keeping you for Himself.

REFLECTION:

How well do you give and receive love? If it's a struggle, what holds you back?

How would having the assurance you are "kept for Christ Jesus" help you give and receive love better?

v. 2 – May mercy, peace, and love be multiplied to you.

I am terrible at math. Not just bad but terrible. My 11-year-old daughter, Anna Kathryn, runs circles around me in regard to basic arithmetic. It's sad really. In fact, I am so bad at math that I am thankful restaurants put recommended tips on receipts now so I don't have to screw up the percentages.

Do you know who is not bad at math? God. He's really good at it. One thing I've learned is God doesn't usually do math by addition, He does it by multiplication. He is always doing exceedingly and abundantly more than we have even thought to ask or can imagine (Ephesians 3:20). And He has infinitely multiplied His mercy toward us who are His beloved.

Here is what I believe is God's favorite equation:

Infinity x Infinity = Infinity

Infinity is any number or amount which is greater than a number or amount you can imagine so if you multiply infinity x infinity then you will get a number or amount you can't imagine. God's mercy and love toward us, His beloved ones, is so far beyond anything we have the capacity to imagine. We don't have the ability to think of its length, depth, or breadth. It is beyond us, and yet, it is set on us.

"But when the kindness of God our Savior and His love for mankind appeared, He saved us, not on the basis of deeds which we have done in righteousness, but according to His mercy, by the washing of regeneration and renewing by the Holy Spirit, whom He poured out upon us richly through Jesus Christ our Savior," – *Titus 3:4-6*

You will never run out of mercy that comes from heaven. The cross of Jesus Christ both propitiates (paid for) and expiates (covered infinitely) our sin. He will never grow tired of filling your bucket with His mercy. And the truth is you can't empty your bucket for him to have to refill it because it's always full.

It's the same with peace and love. He constantly fills us until overflowing. Peace is the pursuit most people are on. They want peace in their lives and minds. For the believer, we have it without end. Peace for us is a person and that person is the infinite King Jesus whose reign will never end and His peace is sure. His kingdom is a kingdom of peace because He is the Prince of Peace (Isaiah 9:6). When we place our trust in Jesus, we have peace without fail or end because He can't fail and He has no end!

I pray, along with Jude, that mercy, peace, and love will be multiplied to you right now. Or better yet, I pray you will walk in the awareness of how mercy, peace, and love have already been multiplied to you infinitely.

REFLECTION:

In what ways has God been filling your bucket with mercy, peace or love this week?

What do you feel like you are lacking that you need to ask God to multiply today?

v. 3 - Beloved, although I was very eager to write to you about our common salvation, I found it necessary to write appealing to you to contend for the faith that was once for all delivered to the saints.

Have you ever been eager to do something and yet knew there was something more pressing that needed to be done before you could do the thing you actually wanted to do? That's what Jude is saying here. He wants to talk about the endless riches of grace which abounds for the Church through the Good News of Jesus Christ, but instead, he has to "contend for the faith." See, in Jude's time, there were severe distortions of the message of Jesus being shared in order to manipulate and deceive people away from the purity of the gospel and persuade them into the ways of religion. Religion is a "do this, not that" set of rules which push you to believe you can do enough, good or bad, to merit God's feelings toward you, but that is not true to the Gospel. The Gospel is an invitation into an abiding personal relationship with your heavenly Father who loves you and sent His Son on a rescue mission to save you.

Our salvation through faith in Jesus Christ guarantees our victory over sin and death for all eternity, and it also guarantees God's enemy is at work against us which means we are in a fight contending for this faith.

"Just because the brilliant Commander in Chief promises victory on the beaches doesn't mean the troops can throw their weapons overboard." – John Piper [3]

A fundamental truth which accompanies being a Jesus follower is we are always at war with an enemy who wants to steal, kill, and destroy us (John 10:10). We don't have the luxury of throwing down our weapons and taking a long nap while we wait for Jesus to finish His mission to rescue sinners and redeem His creation. We have to pick up the armor of God every day to wage war in Jesus' name contending for the faith until the day its fullness is realized.

---

[3] John Piper, "Contend for the Faith," *Desiring God,* November 25, 1984, https://www.desiringgod.org/messages/contend-for-the-faith.

Our faith is threatened every day through conduits such as the media, the higher education system, and generational sin to name a few. It is a truth war and we are in the crucible of human history contending for the Truth who is the person of Jesus Christ. He is not our truth we made up, He is the truth given to us by God and through whom we live and breathe.

This truth was "delivered to all the saints" and is unchanging. The truth we know by name, the Old Testament saints knew by faith. The truth we know by faith is the same truth the apostles saw walk out of that grave in Jerusalem more than 2000 years ago. This truth stands the test of time against all cults and lies which would seek to destroy it. Whether it be the lies of the American dream, the false revelations of the Koran or Book of Mormon, or the temptation to believe the distortions of prosperity as a gospel, it is imperative for the believer to stand on the truth of Jesus Christ. When we do so, we are well equipped to give a defense and wage a Holy war of prayer and preaching against these demonic forces at work. Anyone who claims to have received a new revelation which is in addition to or in opposition to the Word of God given through the prophets and apostles stands in direct opposition to God Himself.

We stand with God and on His Word. Let us not be deceived or led astray but let us hold fast to the sword of truth as we engage our enemy for the glory of our God.

REFLECTION:

How has your faith been threatened in the last month?

In what ways is the Holy Spirit challenging you to contend for the faith? What's your next step in doing so?

v. 4 – For certain people have crept in unnoticed who long ago were designated for this condemnation, ungodly people, who pervert the grace of our God into sensuality and deny our only Master and Lord, Jesus Christ.

The world we live in is a world where feelings have become god, even among many who claim to be God's people. The mantra of modernity is that if it feels right then it must be right. This is the symptom of a cheap grace gospel which is intended to make us feel better, but in the end, if this is believed, it will cost us our souls.

I can't think of a worse indictment than that of being accused of perverting God's grace. Perverting God's grace into sensuality is to submit ourselves unto our feelings as our own master, and in so doing we reject Jesus as our Master. In essence, this means we end up accepting as truth a grace we bestow upon ourselves. But true grace is a grace given to us, without any doing of our own, not a grace we create so our lives can be lived inside the realms of a false sense of peace. Perverted grace is a grace without cost, as the faith hero Dietrich Bonhoeffer writes in his masterpiece, The Cost of Discipleship. "Cheap grace is the preaching of forgiveness without requiring repentance, baptism without church discipline, Communion without confession, absolution without personal confession. Cheap grace is grace without discipleship, grace without the cross, grace without Jesus Christ, living and incarnate." [4]

Any measure of grace which does not begin and end with Jesus Christ is no grace at all. The soul-truth that grace is infinitely costly on the part of Christ is the foundation of what grace is really all about. It cost Him everything and it is this grace we need and it is this costly grace our souls are after. In fact, we want it so badly we would abandon all the measures of this world's success in order to have it for even one second.

In Jesus Christ alone, we receive the full measure of God's grace. A perverted cheap grace points us toward ourselves as the solution to our soul's desires by teaching us to look at our

[4] Dietrich Bonhoeffer, *The Cost of Discipleship* (New York: Macmillian, 1966).

feelings for the answers to soul questions like "Who am I?" and "What on earth am I here for?" But let this not be so of us, my friend.

Let us not look unto ourselves, and thus pervert the grace of God, but let us set our eyes on our Christ Jesus the Lord in and for all things. God's grace given to us through Jesus Christ is what eternally sustains us, and as we experience it we are able to walk in His freedom, mercy, love, and peace.

REFLECTION:

In what ways have you settled for a cheap grace in the past?

If there is something you need God to cover with His endlessly perfect grace, write it down and commit it to prayer today.

v. 5a – Now I want to remind you, although you once fully knew it, that Jesus, who saved...

Jude is talking to people who have renounced their faith and traded truth for a lie. They have abandoned the testimony of the apostles and are making up a new religion which has nothing to do with the truth of Jesus Christ. It is a belief system blending Christianity with cultural preferences. In the days ahead, I will talk more about this apostasy and the judgment which awaits those who ascribe to it, but today I want to focus on the phrase, "I want to remind you" from Jude.

I lose my car keys all the time. You would think that after years of misplacing them I would figure out a better system of keeping up with them, but here we are a few decades into losing them and it still happens on a regular basis. I tend to lose my way too during difficult seasons of life in my walk with Jesus. I'm not saying I get rid of my faith or that my faith can ever leave me, I just lose it as my primary focus because I get distracted by other things which take its place.

Just like my keys aren't truly lost, I just left them somewhere where they are waiting to be found, faith is never truly lost because we didn't give it to ourselves but we can certainly misplace its priority in our lives. And it's easy to do. We get busy, we get lonely, we get fixated on our current circumstances so our faith walk with God becomes an add-on to our lives instead of the reason and purpose for which we live our lives.

When I lose my keys I always try to remember where I was the last time I saw them. In the same way, I often need to slow down and remember my salvation through the gospel and remind myself of the miracles I have seen God do in my life and in the lives of those around me.

Let me remind you today Jesus Christ, who is the second person of the Holy Trinity, was clothed in glory, honor, and righteousness as the King of heaven, and He left His throne to come into this world as a baby boy born to a virgin Jewish girl named Mary. His birth was the fulfillment of dozens of prophecies that foretold a Messiah would one day come to earth to save God's people from their sins. Jesus' birth was the landed invasion of the kingdom of God. This baby boy grew up to be a man who never sinned in action or in intention walking perfectly according to God's standard of living known as the law. As a 30-year-old man, He made Himself and the true kingdom of God known to the world through teachings, miracles, and ministry among the nation of Israel. After 3 years of ministry, He was betrayed so all the prophecies of His coming could be fulfilled and He was murdered brutally on a Roman cross.

God's law (or standard of living) requires perfection and anywhere perfection was not achieved it required that a blood sacrifice be made so those sins could be forgiven. Jesus' perfect blood was shed so our sins could be forgiven. He died so we don't have to.

"For God so loved the world that he gave his only begotten son so that whoever believes in him shall not perish but have everlasting life." – *John 3:16*

This act of forgiveness was made possible through the death of Jesus, and life eternal is made possible because He didn't stay dead. Three days after he was murdered, He rose from the dead and was alive again; He is alive again. This glorious resurrection is the source of eternal life for all who believe in Him, which is to say anyone who believes by faith that Jesus is who He says He is and did what the Bible says He has done can live at peace with God for all eternity.

Jesus died for you. Jesus died instead of you. Jesus died because of you, and me, and all sinners who cannot live up to God's standards of perfection - which is everyone. We don't deserve this gift; we don't deserve Him taking our place; we don't deserve God's love toward us demonstrated on that cross, but while we were still sinners, Christ died for us (Romans 5:8). He did it even though we don't deserve it. That's grace and that's the truth for which we live.

Maybe today the message of the gospel of Jesus Christ finds you in a place where you need a reminder. Maybe you need to be reminded your life is not your own but you have been bought at a price and your life is now hidden with God in Christ Jesus. Faith in Jesus is not something we add to our lives so we get to go to heaven, it is the source from which we live and is what brings heaven to us.

REFLECTION:

Have you abandoned the testimony of the apostles in any area of your life? Take a minute to confess the truth you've exchanged for lies.

How have you seen God's grace at work in the last few weeks?

v. 5b - ...that Jesus who saved a people out of the land of Egypt, afterward destroyed those who did not believe.

Yesterday we were reminded of who Jesus is and what He has done for us. We have the grand luxury of living post the resurrection of Jesus Christ from the dead - as did Jude's audience in the first century. However, his audience was primarily Jewish so bringing to mind the exodus would've been very fitting and a familiar story by which to call them back to the faith. Jude is going back in time reminding them, and us, of God's faithfulness through the generations. In the exodus, God delivers His people from the hands of the tyrant Pharaoh. He saved them from the harsh burden of judgment in the land of Egypt and mercifully led them to and through the wilderness with smoke and fire. He loved them through hardship and protected them from enemies and themselves as he instructed them through Moses and the law. His work on their behalf never ceased but still, they were disobedient and rebelled against Him. Here are a few examples:

- *The people were quick to grumble against God (Exodus 15)*
- *They cowered in fear after hearing the report of the spies to Canaan (Numbers 13)*
- *There was division in the ranks (Numbers 14)*
- *They rebelled against Moses (Numbers 16)*

There are so many more instances we could discuss, but you get the point. The bottom line is despite all God did on their behalf, they still did not trust Him. And unfortunately, anyone who doesn't trust God through Jesus gets exactly what they seek - which is a life without God forever. Life without God forever is destruction and it is the judgment that awaits all those who reject Him. In 1 Cor 10:1-3, Paul writes about those who don't really trust God and their pending separation from God. "For I do not want you to be unaware, brothers, that our fathers were all under the cloud, and all passed through the sea, and all were baptized into Moses in the cloud and in the sea, and all ate the same spiritual food, and all drank the same spiritual drink. For they drank from the spiritual Rock that followed them, and the Rock was Christ. Nevertheless, with most of them God was not pleased, for they were overthrown in the wilderness."

There is no more fearful a place to be than to have experienced God's grace in your life and yet not trust its source, or to have received blessings from God but reject the God who gives them by trusting in ourselves or in another. This is what breaks God's heart as it puts those who don't believe in opposition to Him.

Hebrews 11:6 says, "without faith it is impossible to please God." Faith is the means by which we drink from the Spiritual Rock that is Christ Jesus. Faith is more than agreeing with a statement of facts, it is trusting the whole of your existence into the hands of Christ. It is trusting His death on the cross counted for you and His resurrection from the dead secures you into God's family. It is the willful placing of your dreams, ambitions, weaknesses, desires, money, family, past, and future into the hands of Christ. It is joyfully surrendering to His authority in all things believing His way is better and the outcome of life in His hands is far superior to any version of life we could make up on our own.

Have faith in God today, lean not on your understanding but acknowledge Him in all your ways and He will make your paths straight (Proverbs 3:5-6).

REFLECTION:

In what areas or circumstances of your life do you lack faith in God?

What causes you not to trust that God's love is enough for you to surrender your life to His hands?

v. 6 - ...and the angels who did not stay within their own position of authority, but left their proper dwelling, he has kept in eternal chains under gloomy darkness until the judgment of the great day.

The verse from Jude today sounds scary, right? If not scary, it certainly sounds serious and that's because it is.

In Matthew 25:41 Jesus refers to "...the eternal fire prepared for the devil and his angels" (NIV). And in 2 Peter 2:4 Peter writes, "God spared not the angels that sinned, but cast them down to hell, and committed them to pits of darkness, to be reserved unto judgment." It is not beyond reason to believe Jude is talking about the same. Lucifer and the angels who followed him rejected the purpose for which God created them, and ultimately this is a rejection of God Himself.

I believe Jesus, Peter, and Jude share the reminder of these fallen angels as a warning to us. By rejecting God's rule and reign, which is experienced by living inside God's purpose for creating you, you are rejecting the dignity, purity, and protection that comes with being under God's provision. The fallen angels chose this and would choose it 10,000 times so their fate is sealed under "gloomy darkness."

The difference between men and angels in this regard is that each man didn't choose it for him/herself; it was chosen for us by Adam as Paul writes in Romans 5:12, "just as sin entered the world through one man, and death through sin, and in this way death came to all people, because all sinned." The rejection of God and His purposes were chosen for us through Adam and we continue to choose it for ourselves time and time again through self-reliance and self-righteousness. That is to say, we who were created in God's image to be loved by Him and kept secure under His protection, have rejected our position of authority and left our proper dwelling place. But, praise be to God our Father and the Lord Jesus Christ who has not left us under the gloomy darkness of self-exalting but has stepped out of His proper dwelling place as the King of heaven so He could break us loose from our chains of damnation and replace them with robes of righteousness. Today, by faith, we can live inside God's purpose for creating us and flourish under his rule and reign by trusting in Jesus.

We can trust Jesus in work, in worry, in laughter, and in tears. We can trust Him with our children, money, hurts, and fears. To trust in Jesus is to live as God desires - inside the Father's grand design. Each of us is a unique masterpiece of God's own choosing, and by His grace, we are made alive. He does not leave us to ourselves. He came to save us, secure us for the Father's glory and fame, and to restore us and give us His name. Jesus is higher than the angels so He can do what they could not, and yet He lovingly chose to lower himself beneath us, in order that He might exalt us who are His brothers above the angels forever.

REFLECTION:

What do you need to trust God to do on your behalf today?

v.7 - just as Sodom and Gomorrah and the surrounding cities, which likewise indulged in sexual immorality and pursued unnatural desire

The story of Lot and his family as found in Genesis 19 is one of the saddest and most troubling stories in all of scripture to me. The nastiness of human depravity is on full display as things unfold inside the city gates of Sodom and Gomorrah. God had enough of the wickedness so He acted mercifully to the world and destroyed the cities before their evil could spread any further.

Jude, unlike most who teach or comment on the saga of Sodom and Gomorrah today, makes specific mention of "surrounding cities". We don't know much about the surrounding cities or as Genesis calls them "those cities and all the valley, and all the inhabitants of the cities, and what grew on the ground" (Genesis 19:25), but we do know they were destroyed.

There was, in a very real sense, collateral damage from the sins of Sodom. Everyone has experienced the truth that sin always has collateral damage. In my life, the decades-long shadows of shame that loom over my life from the sins of my youth are an example of the collateral. In our world, we can see the devastating effects of men rejecting their role as fathers and its generational impact. We can see the destruction of marriages due to the consumption of porn and sexual impurity which ravages true love and robs couples of authentic intimacy. We have seen countless times that financial impropriety has long-lasting effects on families, cities, and even nations.

Sin always has collateral damage and it should not be taken lightly. God obviously takes sin so seriously that He "destroyed" His own Son on the cross of Calvary to defeat it. For as horrible as Sodom and Gomorrah's fate was it was only but a foreshadowing of what Jesus was to experience by subjecting Himself to the wrath of God on our behalf. Yes, sin has collateral damage and we should seek holiness in all things.

"If Christ has died for me - ungodly as I am, without strength as I am - then I can no longer live in sin, but must arouse myself to love and serve Him who has redeemed me. I cannot trifle with the evil that killed my best Friend. I must be holy for his sake. How can I live in sin when He has died to save me from it?"
– Charles Spurgeon [5]

We should take seriously our appetites for the sins of the flesh, confess them to Jesus, and trust Him to give us the strength to walk in holiness. In the areas of our lives in which we have not handled our sin in this way, we should run to the throne of God's grace, repent and believe He has forgiven us because He has through Jesus!

As a pastor and a friend to you I want to be sure that like Jude, I highlight the severity of sexual sin. We are all bent toward sexual sin in some way because we are all "carrying fire close to our chest" (Proverbs 6:27). There is nothing capable of producing more shame, robbing more joy or destroying more lives than sexual immorality. When speaking of sexual sin, Jesus said, "If your right eye causes you to sin, take it out and throw it away. It is better to lose one part of your body than to have your whole body thrown into hell. If your right hand causes you to sin, cut it off and throw it away. It is better to lose one part of your body than for your whole body to go into hell" (Matthew 5:29-30). Jesus is pointing to the idea that chasing the fulfillment of sexual desires outside the healthy and holy ways given by God to us through His Word, will leave us in a place that we never intended to go for a lot longer than we want to stay.

For every one drug addict or alcoholic that I've counseled over the years, I have counseled 20 people trapped in sexual sin. In my opinion, the negative impacts throughout history of people practicing sex outside of God's design of one man and one woman for one lifetime, are simply immeasurable. If today you find yourself cuddling up to a secret sexual sin or fantasy I implore you, like James, Jesus' other brother, writes, "Therefore, confess your sins to one another and pray for one another, that you may be healed" (James 5:17).

Read that verse again carefully. It doesn't say confess your sins only to God, it says confess also to one another. When it comes

[5] Charles Haddon Spurgeon, *All of Grace: An Earnest Word with Those who are Seeking Salvation by the Lord Jesus Christ* (United Kingdom: Passmore and Alabaster, 1897).

to sexual sin – or any sin for that matter – the chances that what is kept secret can be healed in secret aren't very good. This kind of sin has to come out into the light by confessing to a trusted person who walks with the Lord. This kind of confession begets the question, "Do you want to be healed?" and I hope your answer is a resounding "YES!!!" If so, run to healing through the powerful bond of confession and repentance. This is an active way to let sin know that you will not be at peace with its presence in your life. Now, you may still be tempted at times but being tempted by sin and cuddling with it are pretty different things.

Take the time today to make the call to a trusted friend who is a believer or a Christian leader in your community and bring what has been hidden in the dark into the light so you can be free in Jesus' name!

REFLECTION:

Ask the Holy Spirit to search your heart. Are you harboring a secret pet sin? If so, who can you confess it to today?

v. 7b – serve as an example by undergoing a punishment of eternal fire.

Sheesh. Another devo on fire and destruction? Are you thinking, "It's getting kind of heavy, my friend"? I know, just hang in there for a minute. Jude is still talking about what happened to Sodom and Gomorrah here and the example we see through their disobedience and God's actions against them. Multiple times Jude and Jesus (Luke 16:19-31, Matthew 25:41) both reference this idea of "eternal fire." It is, in my opinion, also known as the outer darkness, Gehenna, hades, and Sheol. One of the most fundamental teachings of Scripture which must be believed and not forgotten is there is a place where people who have not believed in Jesus will live in torment apart from God forever and this is the just and deserved outcome for everyone. The reality of hell is daunting, heart-breaking, and very sobering. But because we believe in the authority and authenticity of scripture which teaches us about hell, we must discuss how this information is supposed to change us.

One way it changes us is that it should rid us of spiritual complacency. Francis Chan, in his book Erasing Hell, says it like this, "Nothing outside of God and His truth should be sacred to us. And so it is with hell. If hell is some primitive myth left over from conservative tradition, then let's set it on that dusty shelf next to other traditional beliefs that have no basis in Scripture. But if it is true, if the Bible does teach that there is a literal hell awaiting those who don't believe in Jesus, then this reality must change us. It should certainly purge our souls of all complacency." [6] No one who has the love of God in their heart can think about the horrors of an eternity separated from God and not be moved to compassion for all to come to repentance.

Another impact this fundamental truth should have on us is gratitude. It is solely because of Jesus that we will never experience life apart from God. In fact, the Apostle Paul tells us there is nothing that can separate us from God's love that is ours in Christ Jesus (Romans 8:39). Nothing means nothing. It always

[6] Francis Chan, *Erasing Hell: What God Said About Eternity, and the Things We've Made Up* (Colorado Springs, CO: David C. Cook, 2011), 16.

has and always will, so when Paul says that nothing can separate us from the love of God he means there is absolutely nothing that can stop God's love from being lavished on us, His kids, through Christ Jesus.

The opposite of gratitude is entitlement and they can't occupy the same place at the same time so when we get a peek into the riches of God's love toward us the only right response is to be postured in humility. His display of humility toward us perpetuates our display of humility toward Him. Paul writes "God demonstrates," which is to say God puts on display or God makes an example of, "His love toward us in that while we were still sinners, Christ died for us" (Romans 5:8). An example was made of Jesus on the cross so we would be examples of his grace.

We take comfort today that we who are wretched and deserving to be made an example of by punishment of eternal fire have received the free and unconditional gift of God's mercy and are now on display as trophies of His grace for the world to see. May our hearts be filled with gratitude and our lips with praise in response to what Jesus Christ has accomplished on our behalf!

REFLECTION:

Who, in particular, are you moved by compassion for their salvation?

What does it mean to you to be a "trophy of God's grace"?

v. 8 – Yet in like manner these people also, relying on their dreams, defile the flesh, reject authority, and blaspheme the glorious ones.

Each of us, at different times in our lives, finds ourselves in a struggle with those in authority over us. This could include politicians, government officials, teachers, coaches, bosses, parents, or leaders of any sort. And it is often in this struggle with authority that our true character is revealed. In the case of the impostors, Jude was warning the Church about, they certainly rejected all spiritual authority in the Church creating much discord among the brethren. If you peel back all the layers of their sedition you see a base desire for self-defined freedom. They want to live free of anyone's rule or reign in their life and want to be lord of their own life. This rejection of God's sovereign rule and reign over everything is what the Bible calls blasphemy. Blasphemy is commonly taught as the "unforgivable sin" because it is the rejection of God. It is a life lived on purpose in the interest of self-glorification.

True freedom is the ability to do whatever you want to without ever feeling guilt or shame. This is the freedom that Christ offers us. Freedom in Christ is doing whatever He wants us to do and knowing He will never put us to shame or create any guilt. The longer we walk with Him the more our wants conform to His wants and the deeper we walk in this freedom. Heaven is where this freedom will be lived unrestricted for all eternity.

You may ask, "Am I truly free if my freedom is found by doing what someone else wants me to do?" The answer is, YES! The reason it is true freedom is that what He wants for us is far more than we could ever want for ourselves. His plans for us are so far superior to anything we could conjure up. This freedom comes with uncontested joy, unmatched desire, an incredible opportunity, and absolutely no regrets. Jesus says, "If the Son has set you free, you will be free indeed" (John 8:36). We will never find any version of true freedom in ourselves. It is only through the Son that we have absolute freedom in every layer of life.

In Christ Jesus, we are free from,
Free from the power of sin and death.
Free from our past failures.
Free from the chains of our self-pity.
Free from enslavement to insecurity or pride.
Free from a life alone.
Free from the bottomless pursuit of self.
Free from the lies of the evil one.
Free from the generational sins handed down to us.
Free from the wage of sin.
Free from the corruption of the will.

In Christ Jesus, we are free to,
Free to walk in the joy that has been set before us.
Free to live patiently with ourselves and others.
Free to believe the gospel and walk in its power.
Free to be healed and bring healing.
Free to love God with all of our heart, soul, mind, and strength.
Free to walk with God.
Free to love others as we love ourselves.
Free to share all we have joyfully.
Free to submit ourselves under God's rule and reign through
    Jesus' Lordship.
Free to live for God's glory and its infinite worth.
Free to trust in Christ's forgiveness.
Free to be more than a conqueror.
Free. Completely. Free.

REFLECTION:

In what ways have you tried to be lord over your own life?

What do you need Christ to free you from today?

v. 9 - But when Michael, contending with the devil, was disputing the body of Moses, he did not presume to pronounce a blasphemous judgment, but said, "The Lord rebuke you."

What an interesting verse! This is the only place in the entirety of scripture that makes mention of this supernatural contest between Michael and Satan. Jude is putting forth that after God Himself had Moses buried after his death (Deuteronomy 34:5-6) Satan wanted to do something different with the body. Maybe Satan wanted to reveal the burial place of Moses to the nation of Israel so the people could idolize it or make it sacred in an unholy manner. Perhaps he was contending against Moses being allowed into heaven because he had committed murder or because of his disobedience at Meribah which cost him entry into the promised land. We don't know exactly what Satan's agenda was, but whatever the details are, they are not nearly as important as the fact that there is an ongoing contest in which the angels of God's army are contending against God's enemies on behalf of God's people.

If you are a Bible-believing Jesus follower there is absolutely no denying the reality of angels and their role in fulfilling God's commands. I have never seen an angel though I trust some people who say they have, I don't believe in angels because of what I have personally seen but because of what the Bible says. There is an almost endless number of accounts of them throughout Scripture. John the revelator writes that there are 10,000 x 10,000 angels in the throne room ministering to the Lamb (Revelation 15:11) and King David writes that God's chariots are 20,000 with thousands of angels (Psalm 68:17).

Billy Graham talks about the work of angels in this way: "Angels belong to a uniquely different dimension of creation which we, limited to the natural order, can scarcely comprehend. God has given angels higher knowledge, power, and mobility than us. They are God's messengers whose chief business is to carry out His orders in the world." [7]

---

[7] Billy Graham, *Graham 2in1 - Angels: God's Secret Angels / Peace with God* (Nashville, TN: Thomas Nelson, 2009), 17.

Angels are fascinating creations of God's design and worth ample time in study and learning, but today I want to encourage you with this truth; there are angels watching over you just as Michael was watching over Moses.

In 1 Corinthians 4:9, Paul writes, "For I think that God has exhibited us, apostles, as last of all, like men sentenced to death, because we have become a spectacle to the world, to angels, and to men."

Paul, no stranger to the divine action of God's righteous angels as well as those of the deviant fallen angels, reminds us here that angels are watching. God's good angels, created for His work and to carry out His Word, are pulling for you and want to see you flourish according to God's plan for your life. I believe these angels are fully aware of all the splendor of God's kingdom and want us to experience it in every way. It is and should be a comfort to us that God loves us so much He has tasked divine warriors of light to care for and watch over us.

REFLECTION:

What account of angels in Scripture brings you comfort or peace?

When have you sensed the oversight and protection of God through an angel?

v. 10 - But these people blaspheme all that they do not understand, and they are destroyed by all that they, like unreasoning animals, understand instinctively.

Jude continues his railing against the false teachers who are leading the Church astray. They are doing this by changing the pure Gospel message of Jesus Christ as given through the apostles into a twisted message of "do what you want based on how you feel." Here, in verse 10, Jude asserts the fact that following our own desires will lead us to a place of ruin apart from God's love and kindness. This is the same conclusion the apostle Paul declares in Romans 1:18-25.

"For the wrath of God is revealed from heaven against all ungodliness and unrighteousness of men who by their unrighteousness suppress the truth. For what can be known about God is plain to them, because God has shown it to them. For in his invisible attributes, namely, his eternal power and divine nature, have been clearly perceived, ever since the creation of the world, in the things that have been made. So they are without excuse. For although they knew God, they did not honor him as God or give thanks to him, but they became futile in their thinking, and their foolish hearts were darkened. Claiming to be wise, they became fools and exchanged the glory of the immortal God for images resembling mortal man and birds and animals and creeping things. Therefore God gave them up in the lusts of their hearts to impurity, to the dishonoring of their bodies among themselves, because they exchanged the truth about God for a lie and worshiped and served the creature rather than the Creator, who is blessed forever! Amen."

Jude and Paul alike remind us the eternal goal of our enemy and the determined outcome of our sinful nature is at its foundation the suppression of truth. Inside the truth, which is the person of Jesus Christ as the revealed glory of God made manifest to us, there is freedom, hope, and eternal life. The truth of Jesus is what sin and Satan suppress by means of distraction and discontentment as well as pagan religion and blatant attack on God's existence. Whether the deceptions be subtle or obvious, the end goal is the same - to suppress the truth. As surrendered agents of grace, we have the sword of the spirit to fight back against the fiery darts of truth suppression, and we do this by taking every wayward thought and every lust-filled temptation and making them captive to the Word of God (2 Corinthians 10:5).

As Jesus was tempted on the Mount of Temptation, He uttered these words, "...It is written..." in His combat against the temptations of Satan to abandon His first love (Matthew 4:1-11). We follow His example by declaring "it is written" as we hold steadfast to the truth of God's plan and the promises of God's love in our lives.

The three most important words echoed into the eternity of the believer are Jesus' cry from the cross: "It is finished.' And the three most important words ever uttered by Jesus for the believer in this life are "It is written." These words have Spirit-filled power to help you overcome.

When the enemy rises up to lie to you, do not let him suppress the truth.

When he says: "You're not good enough."

You say: "You're dang right I'm not good enough, but God said in Romans 8:1 that there is no condemnation for those who are in Christ Jesus and I am in Christ Jesus so be gone Satan."

When he says: "You're still guilty."

You say: "I hear you. I was guilty, but Romans 3:21-26 says all fall short of Gods glory but I am justified by His grace and redeemed by Jesus through faith. This shows God's divine forbearance that He has passed over the former things and His righteousness is now mine."

When he says: "Why don't you chase those feelings of lust so you will be happier?"

You say: "I don't have to do that because just like Psalms 119:11 says, I have hidden God's word in my heart so that I might not sin against Him, and according to Psalms 101:3 I will not set anything wicked before my eyes."

When he says: "You are your past."

You say: "Get behind me Satan because 2 Corinthians 5:17 says in Christ Jesus I am a new creation, the old has passed and the new has come."

When he says: "Be afraid."

You say: "I will not! In 2 Timothy 1:7 God said that He didn't give me a spirit of fear but of love and power and a sound mind."

When he says: "You are unlovable."

You say: "God said in Romans 8:35-39 that nothing can separate me from the love of Christ - not tribulation, or persecution, or famine, or nakedness, or danger, or sword. In all things we are more than conquerors through Him who loved us. Neither death nor life, nor angels nor things to come, nor powers, nor height nor depth nor anything else in all creation will be able to separate us from the love of God in Christ Jesus our Lord."

When he says: "Love this world and the things in it."

You say: "I will not and I don't have to love anything other than my God. Paul says in Colossians 3:1 that I am raised with Christ and I will seek the things that are above, where Christ is, seated at the right hand of God. I will set my mind on things above, not on things that are on earth."

REFLECTION:

In what way has the enemy tried to suppress the truth from you in the last week?

What truth of God's Word do you need to declare over the enemy today?

v. 11 - Woe to them! For they walked in the way of Cain...

Cain really made a mess of things. What was in his heart made itself clear when he killed his brother. And years later, a very serious indictment against a Jew in the 1st century would've been to be accused of walking in the way of Cain. Envy and anger seeped from Cain's pores as he looked upon God's acceptance of his brother's gift and the simultaneous rejection of his gift.

"Abel, on his part also brought the firstborn of his flock and of their fat portions. And the Lord had regard for Abel and for his offering, but for Cain and for his offering He had no regard so Cain was very angry, and his face fell." – *Genesis 4:4-5*

Firstborns, first fruits, and firstlings are common uses of "first" phrasings throughout all of scripture, and there is certainly a good reason for it. What Cain failed to grasp is that in Abel's heart God is first and He can't and won't be second. He is first in placement as well as in priority which means we don't "put" God first in our lives but that He is first in all things so we must order our lives around His firstness. If we don't do this, our lives will be out of order. Our families, finances, schedules, efforts, and energies are in line with God's peace-filled kingdom wherever and whenever He is first.

The New Testament expression of this firstness is fully revealed in and through Jesus Christ as Paul writes to the church in Colosse: "He is the image of the invisible God, the firstborn of all creation. For by him all things were created, in heaven and on earth, visible and invisible, whether thrones or dominions or rulers or authorities—all things were created through him and for him. And he is before all things, and in him all things hold together. And he is the head of the body, the church. He is the beginning, the firstborn from the dead, that in everything he might be preeminent. For in him all the fullness of God was pleased to dwell, and through him to reconcile to himself all things, whether on earth or in heaven, making peace by the blood of his cross" (Colossians 1:15-20).

Paul's statement that Jesus is preeminent is a way of saying He is first. He is "before all things" as Paul states it. Jesus is heaven's first and best. He is the first fruits, first born, only begotten of God, and He was given for us as a sacrifice for our sin so we might be pleasing unto God. Accordingly, we should love Him with our first and best. God doesn't accept leftovers or second place in our lives; He demands and deserves to be first.

The invitation of grace we receive by way of Jesus' sacrifice on the cross is to surrender all the parts of our lives under the firstness of God and to orient ourselves around His promises and provisions. In doing so, we get to walk in His blessings.

On the contrary, to walk in the way of Cain is to treat God as a second-rate citizen in the home of our hearts. Let us walk in the way of Jesus, choosing to see and accept God as first in all things as we joyfully align ourselves with the abundance of His Word.

REFLECTION:

In what areas of your life do you need to re-align under God as first?

What needs to change to make that happen?

v. 11b - ....and abandoned themselves for the sake of gain to Balaam's error and perished in Korah's rebellion.

Jude connects 3 events in verse 11, the way of Cain (Gen 4), Balaam's error (Numbers 22-24), and Korah's rebellion (Numbers 16). We can be sure Jude wasn't pulling any punches in battling against the rampant false teaching and teachers of his day because the people he is comparing them to are beyond shameful in the history of Israel. "Them are fighting words" is how we would've said it where I grew up.

Something very interesting stands out to me in the second half of verse 11 when Jude says, "...and abandoned themselves for the sake of gain...". What does it mean to abandon yourself? And more so to do it for the sake of gain?

You are complex. There is no one like you and never has been. You are uniquely designed by God for His glory and your joy. You won't ever be repeated; you are you and no one else can be you. God created you in His image with dignity, honor, self-respect, and purpose. This means to abandon yourself means to leave all the reasons God created you along with the uniqueness you bring to the world.

What would ever make someone want to abandon all that beauty and quality craftsmanship? The allure of power would. The desire for power is so subtle. In all 3 of Jude's examples, you see men grabbing for the immediate satisfaction of power, and all of them - and many others - suffer the consequences.

I've never met someone who just outright says, "I want more power," but I have seen and lived the behavior that being power-hungry produces, which is control. We want control of the situations in our lives because on some subconscious or maybe even conscious level, it makes us feel better. The truth is we want to be God, not over everything, just over what we think are our things.

This struggle for control is often what makes marriage and parenting so difficult. We find ourselves in power struggles against ourselves and other sinners like us and we don't recognize it for what it is – a tactic of the enemy to leave us grasping for whatever we can take or manufacture on our own. And the true deceit of power is we actually get convinced in our minds that we are doing the right thing. The gain we are after in these situations is to be right in our mind as Proverbs 21:2-3 says: "Every way of a man is right in his own eyes, but the Lord weighs the heart. To do righteousness and justice is more acceptable to the Lord than sacrifice."

To walk in the way of Jesus is to open our hands and let go of control by putting our trust in Him. This is truly surrendering our control to the one who actually has it in all things at all times. This is a daily, willful, practice that its gains are wisdom, maturity, and unexplainable peace.

REFLECTION:

In what ways have you been guilty of being "right in your own eyes"?

Where do you need to let go of control today?

v. 12 – these are hidden reefs at your love feasts, as they feast with you without fear, shepherds feeding themselves, waterless clouds, swept along by the wind, fruitless trees in late autumn, twice dead, uprooted.

In the early church, they often gathered and shared a meal of fellowship called love feasts or agapais. Agapais is the plural of agape which is the Greek word for unconditional love. [8] These feasts were designed for believers to remind one another of the unconditional love they have from God and for each other. It seems that apostates – which are people who renounce the faith or abandon the core tenants of the faith and are convinced in their own minds they are right and want others to agree with them - had slithered their way into these feasts and were being welcomed by the Church to do so.

Jude says these men are without fear and then lists all the ways in which they are practicing self-indulgence. The distinction that they "are without fear" sounds like an odd strike against someone's character. Today, if someone would say that you are without fear that would be a compliment. We champion bravery and courage and rightfully preach Jesus' words when He says, "I have said these things to you, that in me you may have peace. In the world you will have tribulation. But take heart; I have overcome the world" (John 16:33). We also hold fast to this command: "For God gave us a spirit not of fear but of power and love and self-control" (2 Timothy 1:7).

As students of scripture, we can sometimes come upon ideas which seem competitive like the countless instructions to "not be afraid" and then the counsel to "fear the Lord" on top of texts like our main text for today where a lack of fear is considered to be a serious character deficiency. This can be confusing, but it's in these instances of study where we have to remind ourselves of whom the author is speaking to and what the context is as he pens the words because we know God's Word cannot contradict itself and He cannot lie.

---

[8] *Englishman's Concordance,* s.v. "unconditional love," *Bible Hub,* accessed March 2, 2022, https://biblehub.com/greek/agapais_26.htm.

God's Word says "to fear the Lord is the beginning of wisdom" (Proverbs 9:10). This reverent fear of the almighty God does not cause us, His children, to shy away from Him but to approach Him humbly. In fact, we have no reason to fear anything other than the Lord because He alone has made us more than conquerors through Christ Jesus (Romans 8:37). That is good news for the believer.

On the other hand, the unbeliever, and especially the liars and deceivers who are wolves preying among the sheep of God's church, have much to be afraid of. Like a fruitless tree in late autumn that is twice dead and uprooted, unbelievers will show themselves to be spiritually dry and their words brittle and untrustworthy in due time. Character is always revealed. There is no way to hide who you are behind closed doors forever, and it is God's goodness to us and all the world that He is at work to expose darkness by bringing it to light. While I highly doubt you would consider yourself a false teacher practicing self-indulgence through the intentional deception of God's people, perhaps you have believed lies you thought were true.

I have a question for you: Who has the loudest voice in your life? Who do you take your spiritual guidance from? I hope it is someone committed to God's Word. Many people offer flattering and easy-to-believe advice, but when you examine it and hold it up to God's Word, you'll actually find it is in direct contrast to His truth – the best source of wisdom and direction for life.

I'd encourage you to spend time today and pray something like this:

"Search me, O God, and know my heart! Try me and know my thoughts! And see if there be any grievous way in me, and lead me in the way of the everlasting!" – *Psalm 139:23-24*

REFLECTION:

Who are the God-fearing, trustworthy voices you can rely on to help you discern God's truth?

When you asked God to search you to see if there is any grievous way in you, what did His Spirit reveal?

v. 13 - wild waves of the sea, casting up the foam of their own shame; wandering stars, for whom the gloom of utter darkness has been reserved forever.

Have you ever watched a star wander? Where do they wander off to? When stars shoot across the sky, do they not just disappear into the black nothingness of space? With very potent visuals Jude reminds us here that nature teaches us much about how God works. He cares about details and He paints with a very fine brush to make sure everything is just as He designed it.

Whitecaps on waves show us many things but two things they give us is a way to perceive how tall the wave is, and when deep out at sea they show us which way the wind is blowing. When you know what to look for, this detail tells you much about the waters you are trying to navigate. For example, when large waves crash against a shoreline, they leave behind them a foam of sorts, kind of like a remnant until the next wave comes to wash it away and do the same. Just like waves we can sit and watch for hours, every detail reveals something to us about the God who created the ocean and purposed the waves.

In the same way, because God made us in His image, we have inherited His penchant for detail. What is underneath the surface spills out through words, facial expressions, and repeated patterns of behavior. In the case of Jude's enemies, it would seem shame and pain were spilling out of them because of their chosen path.

The undertow of the current of our lives is very strong, and at times it can feel like a rip tide dragging us toward our destination. For many of us, we have pain or grief under the surface we have yet to deal with, and it's pulling us toward a shore of loneliness. Others are harboring unforgiveness and just can't release the wrongs which have been done to us.

Just like the way God designed the waves and stars, there is a created order for everything. All things that have been created by sin are heading in a direction away from God and His endless riches of grace while all things that have been given by grace are leading toward God and His enduring kingdom. There may be times in life when we feel like we are being pulled in both directions - like we are stuck in some cosmic tug of war - but the good news is that for the believer, the "foam of our shame" was cast upon the cross of Jesus Christ. Shame has left a remnant on the shores of our earthly existence, but the waves of Christ's blood which washes away those remnants are washing away any shadow of shame that may exist.

May we not shy away from His waves of mercy but instead, may we run as fast as we can into them and let them wash us clean.

REFLECTION:

What pain, grief or unforgiveness do you need to deal with?

How has the enemy been using shame to keep you from fully experiencing the power of the cross?

v. 14 – It was also about these that Enoch, the seventh from Adam, prophesied,

Enoch would be a very familiar name to Jews in the first century. He was father to Methuselah and the Bible says he lived 365 years and "he walked with God, and he was not, for God took him" (Genesis 5:24). There has been much debate by scholars over Jude referring to Enoch's prophecy. Some claim that because Jude quotes Enoch his writings should be included in the Bible. I think this is silly for 2 reasons: First, if Enoch's writings were divinely inspired and supposed to be in the biblical canon they would be because God is sovereign. He simply would not allow something in His Word that wasn't supposed to be there. Second, if the fact that Jude quoted Enoch makes his writings divinely inspired then it could easily be argued that we would have to include others like Aratus and Cleanthes since Paul quotes them in Acts 17. After all, canonization was based on a number of factors, including the authorship of an apostle, prophet, or a close associate of the apostles, the truthfulness of the book and alignment with previously accepted canonical books, the acceptance of Christ Himself, and the edification of the Church over time. I find this debate to be a good reminder to me how silly Christians can be sometimes, and how we often make stuff up to argue about amongst ourselves.

If you were a Jew receiving this letter from Jude and you saw Enoch's name you would certainly recognize it and it would invoke a response from you because the testimony of his life and departure from earth was the stuff of legends. The Bible says Enoch walked with God and was taken by God to heaven. It doesn't say, "he died", it says, "God took him." The fact God took Him implies that he lived faithfully in intimacy with God serving his purpose until God took him to heaven. Whether he died or was taken up by God alive is a question we can ask one day when we are in heaven, but for today I want to remind you of the importance of having a legacy of faith like that of Enoch.

I imagine his faith legacy would've been inspiring to Jude's readers, as it should be. Jude did not quote Enoch solely to bring merit to the warnings we have read to this point in his letter but also to remind his readers that faithfulness like that of Enoch is required and rewarded. It is very tempting today to take shortcuts in life, to try and finish first at all costs, or to do just enough to get by, but that is not the call of the believer in Jesus. Believers are rewarded for being good and faithful (Matthew 25:23).

One of the marks of the faithful is perseverance. Perseverance means to stay the course, don't give up, don't walk away, don't take the easy way or be lazy, but to stay in constant pursuit of holiness through faithfully following Jesus' instruction and lifestyle.

I have never considered abandoning my faith, but I have been tempted around every corner to be less than faithful in walking worthy of the calling which I have received. I have been tempted to settle for far less than immeasurably more than I could think or imagine in my life, but I know I would forsake the abundant life God has for me in doing so. Remembering this and subjecting myself to the Holy Spirit's rule and reign in my life helps me stay the course.

Today, Enoch can serve as a reminder for us of the importance and the blessing that comes with being faithful to Christ in all things. I wonder if there are areas of our lives in which we have let monotony, apathy, complacency, anger, or sloth take hold resulting in the loss of our perseverant spirit. If you find this to be true, I encourage you to spend some time on your knees asking God to restore to you the joy of your salvation and to forge in you a spirit of steadfastness so you can joyfully serve Him with gladness in your heart.

REFLECTION:

Is there an area in your life in which you struggle to persevere? If so, what is it and what makes it hard for you?

What do you hope will be your legacy of faith?

v. 14 cont'd – "Behold, the Lord comes with ten thousands of his holy ones, to execute judgment on all and to convict all the ungodly of all their deeds of ungodliness that they have committed in such an ungodly way, and of all the harsh things that ungodly sinners have spoken against him."

Jude, having grown up in a Jewish household, was very educated in the values and traditions of the Jewish people. This quote from Enoch in verse 14 would have certainly been esteemed by many of those in the early church as meaningful because of who said it and when it was said. Enoch lived before the flood of Noah's time and for his words to travel through oral tradition for thousands of years meant they were highly regarded. The point of quoting Enoch, however, is not to merit Enoch's words as God-inspired but to draw attention to something Enoch knew. "Ungodly." "Ungodliness." "Ungodly way." "Ungodly sinners." These are the ways Enoch describes people who speak against God and defame His glorious name. God holds His name in the highest regard and this is really really good news.

What's in a name? I have to believe it's more than just letters or a helpful piece of language so we have something more eloquent than "Hey you!" to say to each other. Merriam-Webster says the essential meaning of a name is: a word or phrase constitutes the distinctive designation of a person or thing. [9] Interesting. Is it enough to say that a name is a group of letters that when spoken initiates the expectancy of a response from the individual being referenced? I'm not sure it is. I think names are more valuable than that. After all, your name carries with it your history, your natural identity, your heritage, your known mistakes, and your known triumphs. If your name comes up in a group of people who know you, each of them has a different thought that pops into their mind about who you are. Every name carries weight with it, so it is worth infinitely more than merely a verbal calling card.

---

[9] *Merriam-Webster*, s.v. "name," accessed March 2, 2022, https://www.merriam-webster.com/dictionary/name.

The weightiest and most important name to ever cross humans' imagination is "YHWH". You see, God, in His name – Yahweh – has revealed His essence. YHWH is considered the most sacred name of God to the Israelites. The Hebrew letters are yodh, he, waw, and he. When those letters are placed together it forms what is known as the tetragrammaton and represents the name God gave Himself when speaking to Moses on Mt. Sinai in Exodus 3. [10] When it is spoken, an effect that is much like breathing happens in our lungs. His name is unlike any other name, and He is the only one who can handle the pressure of having such a name. He takes His name – and the significance of its meaning to us - very, very seriously, and this is good news because if at any point God held anything in higher regard than His own name He would cease to be God. Something or someone else would be responsible for sustaining all created things, and no one can handle that eternal task except the ever-present, all-powerful YHWH God!

"To know God's names is to experience His nature, and that level of intimacy is reserved for those who humbly depend on Him. God will not share His glory with another. We must humble ourselves if we really want to know Him. We must realize our insignificance before we can recognize the significance that comes only through Him. We are to hallow His name and His name alone. You can't know His names until you forget your own." – Tony Evans [11]

REFLECTION:

What do you think your name means to others? To God?

What is one of God's names that you are focusing on or should be focusing on in this season of life?

---

[10] Philip Graham Ryken, *Exodus: Saved for God's Glory* (Wheaton, IL: Crossway Books, 2015), 538.

[11] Tony Evans, *Praying Through the Names of God* (Eugene, OR: Harvest House Publishers, 2014), 18.

v. 16 – These are grumblers,

Without fail, our words always reveal what is going on inside us. Jesus says that "Out of the heart, the mouth speaks" (Matthew 12:34). And James, the other brother, says, "The tongue is a fire, a world of unrighteousness" (James 3:6).

Words have power and they reveal whose power we are relying on for strength in life. The apostates that Jude is warring against are "grumblers," which means they use the words to sow discontent and discord among the saints. Words have the power to effect change and the grumblings of these deceivers in the early church were bringing about negative change inside the Church.

Grumbling has an inside-out ability to rob joy from a person. To grumble is to give voice to the low rumble of angst and selfishness that lies just below the surface of an unsatisfied soul. It's a quick word against someone for no apparent reason, it's a tense tone to your spouse because they ask for your help, it's an undue harsh verbal lash to your children when they don't listen the first time. Grumbling comes out of the mouth of the heart that is not happy in God.

Have you ever spent time with someone who never seems to be happy? Maybe you've spent a lot of time with someone like that because if you were honest, you'd have to admit that person is you. It is exhausting to be around a grumbler, and it is even more exhausting on the soul to be one. Grumbling has a way of deepening sadness not relieving it and heaping pain onto pain not healing it. Grumbling has a way of closing our minds to the truth and instead opening it to lies.

I have experienced seasons of feeling joylessness in my life, even as a believer, and in those seasons, I found the easiest thing to do was to find something to grumble about. It's as if the joyless heart believes by voicing its joylessness and inviting others into said joylessness, it will somehow be able to produce a moment's joy for itself. This is not true. Gratitude produces joy and joy produces gratitude. Grumbling can never produce joy because it doesn't come from joy.

Sometimes the best thing we can do to measure joy is to pause and self-reflect on the condition of our soul, and the quickest way to investigate soul health is by taking inventory of our words and tone of voice. If you are a believer in Jesus the Christ but are experiencing a repeated pattern of joylessness, check your words and see what is spilling out.

REFLECTION:

What are you grateful for today?

What spills out in your words – joy or joylessness?

v. 16 - malcontents,

Have you ever wanted what you didn't have? Have you ever wanted to be somewhere in life you weren't? We all have. I call it the "myth of there" and we all buy into it from time to time. It is the idea that if we can just get "there" we will finally be content. If we can just get a certain amount of money in the bank account, or that promotion at work, or that relationship started, or that co-worker to leave, or our kids to change or, or, or, or...... then we will get "there."

To be malcontent is to be unsatisfied with who you are, where you are, and what God's given you. The myth of there is one of the most peddled lies that comes out of the modern version of the American dream. The inherent right of each person to equally have life, liberty, and share in the pursuit of happiness has become, at least in America, the entitled belief that each man should be handed whatever life they want without any restrictions while being free to do whatever they want without consequence and pursue happiness as an end instead of a means. It is safe to say we have lost our way, but for the believer in Jesus, this should not be the case. So often in the west, we confuse our identity as Americans with our identity as Christians. We have, in a lot of ways, created a blended belief system between the ideals of our nation and doctrines of scripture. This confusion has created more malcontent amongst believers than anything else I've encountered. We are so often trapped between our American measure of success and our desire to be faithful to God, and they rarely line up. We talk a big faith game but when it comes down to it we are more worried about our 401k's than we are our souls' happiness in God. We have lost who we are and where we are, and we need to be reminded of what we have already been given.

If you are reading this and have placed your trust in Jesus Christ as your Lord and repented of sin, you are now a child of God. That is who you are and it should inform you how to view yourself and the world now. The old you has (and is) passed away and the new you has and is here to stay forever

(2 Corinthians 5:17). This is not something you have done for yourself; it is something God has done for you and is doing to you.

"But God, being rich in mercy, because of the great love with which he loved us, even when we were dead in our trespasses, made us alive together with Christ—by grace you have been saved— and raised us up with him and seated us with him in the heavenly places in Christ Jesus." (Ephesians 2:4-6)

You have been seated in the heavenlies in Christ Jesus. That is where you are. And last, but certainly not least, is what you have been given:

"For God gave us a spirit not of fear but of power and love and self-control." (2 Timothy 1:7)

"For you did not receive the spirit of slavery to fall back into fear, but you have received the Spirit of adoption as sons, by whom we cry, 'Abba! Father!'" (Romans 8:15)

"For who has understood the mind of the Lord so as to instruct him? But we have the mind of Christ." (1 Corinthians 2:16)

These verses detail only a few of the thousands of gifts you have received through God's grace. Be who you are, be where you are, and rejoice today in what you have been given. You need not go "there" to find joy and contentment because joy and contentment came here to find you through Christ Jesus our Lord.

REFLECTION:

In what ways have you bought into the "myth of there"?

What are three things you have been given because of the grace of God that you can rejoice in today?

v. 16 - following their own sinful desires;

Followers follow. That's deep stuff right there. Inherent to being a follower is following. We follow the laws of the land, or at least most of us try to most of the time. We follow Siri when she says to turn. We follow directions when we want to do something right the first time. We do all of these things because it is hardwired into us that we are followers.

To follow means to "come after in time or order". [12] It is to be lined up behind something with the intention of staying there. When it comes to the direction of our lives, we have two choices: follow Jesus or follow our own sinful desires. It's really that simple.

In New Testament times, a rabbi would call an apprentice to follow him and that apprentice would leave his life as he knew it to follow closely behind the rabbi. And when he departed his old life to pursue this new life of following, a blessing of "May you be covered with the dust of your rabbi" would be spoken over him. The expectation of this kind of following is that he would walk so closely that the dust the rabbi kicked up would get all over him.

This is the same call Jesus had on the first four disciples on the beaches of the Sea of Galilee. He said, "Come and follow me" and follow him they did! It is also the same call He has given to each of us as His followers. He asks us to pick up all of who we are and follow Him closely. In other words, He invites us to be covered in His dust.

There are three things at work in the life of those who truly follow Jesus. They may not all be at work at the same time, and they may not work themselves out in the same manner or with the same vigor, but if you look into the sprouting seeds of faith inside the believer, you will certainly find them at work.

One reality you are certain to find in the life of the believer is the conviction for sin. To be a Jesus follower is to be indwelt by His

---

[12] *Merriam-Webster*, s.v. "follow," accessed March 2, 2022, https://www.merriam-webster.com/dictionary/follow.

spirit and that spirit is calling and equipping us to walk in line with Jesus. Anywhere we get out of step, He shows us so we can find our way back into our rabbi's dust.

The second thing we find at work in the life of a believer is a hunger to know more. Peter, one of the original disciples, tells us "His divine power has granted to us all things that pertain to life and godliness, through the knowledge of him who called us to his own glory and excellence" (2 Peter 1:3). This means we have everything we need in God's Word and from God's spirit to walk out in the life to which Jesus has called us. And the more we follow in His steps, the more we want to know about what He has said and how we can follow Him more closely.

The third condition we find at work in the true follower of Jesus is a passion for others to follow Him. There is plenty of room in line behind Jesus and He throws up a lot of dust to cover the multitudes, so we dare not covet or crowd His call. Instead, we share it freely with others because we want them to taste the same depths of His teachings, the hope of His life, and the power of His resurrection as we have.

REFLECTION:

What sin has the Holy Spirit convicted you of lately?

Are you hungry to know God more deeply? Does your quiet time reflect a healthy appetite for the things of God?

Do you find yourself feeling passionate about reaching the lost? If not, why?

v. 16 - they are loud mouthed boasters,

To boast is to verbally bring attention to something you have or have done for your own self-satisfaction. To be a loudmouth is to make sure that you've said it enough times and, in enough ways, to be sure you are heard. Being a loud-mouthed boaster is a sure-fire way to choke out healthy relationships and lose the perspective of a God-honoring worldview. We live in a world where we are almost shamed into believing we have to assert ourselves if we want to be noticed, and we have to be loud on social media and garner a following in order to have influence. We are constantly being fed the false narrative that attention is the same thing as significance.

The call of Jesus is the exact opposite in every way. He calls us to blessed self-forgetfulness, not to the pursuit of self-seeking attention. Jesus says, "Blessed are the meek" (Matthew 5:5) not blessed is the one who has the most fans or likes. Meek does not mean weak. Meekness is bridled strength; think of a purebred stallion with a bit in its mouth that is strong but under control. The horse is powerful but not reckless. We should be wary of the self-aggrandizing loudmouths of this world because the louder someone is on behalf of themselves or their opinion the more likely there is a deep hurt below the surface which may cause a spirit of division.

Many times in my life I have traded being faithful to God for being noticed by people. I have been quick to share my opinion and slow to listen to others. I can only think of 1 or 2 times in my life when I have regretted not saying something I thought. I can think of 10,000 times when I have regretted saying what I thought. It is ever tempting to want to put yourself forward for a quick affirmation or to tell a story in which you are the central character. I have found, though, that the end result of boasting in any form, whether by being loud-mouthed or by a more subtle means, provides a brief moment of satisfaction that is quickly followed by the return of a deeper longing. No matter how much affirmation is given toward our efforts of self-exaltation in a physical or digital world, it can never be enough to fill our soul's empty spaces.

Paul writes, "But far be it from me to boast except in the cross of our Lord Jesus Christ, by which the world has been crucified to me, and I to the world" (Galatians 6:14).

I offer Paul's words as a prayer for us and as a guide to our words. We will never regret making the cross of Jesus Christ the centerpiece of our conversations with God or with each other. The best way for us to walk in blessed self-forgetfulness is to willfully and verbally make much of Jesus Christ and His cross. In doing so we nail ourselves to that cross for the freedom of death to self. To be dead to this world and for this world to be dead to us is to be truly free, fully alive, and able to see there is only One name worth boasting and it is the name by which all people under heaven can be saved.

REFLECTION:

When was the last time you felt tempted to seek attention or boast of your accomplishments?

What is the deeper longing that was being neglected?

In what way can you make Jesus the centerpiece of your conversations and efforts today?

v. 16 - showing favoritism to gain advantage.

It is tempting to position yourself in such a way that people who you believe have power will see you and reward you. Tim Keller once said something like, "You know that money has power over you when you treat people in a different economic class than you differently than someone in your class."[13] He uses money but I think the same is true for power or position and often these things go together. If you treat someone who has more money or power than you differently than you treat a peer who has the same or less money or power than you, you are showing favoritism. And to do so for selfish gain is to place yourself squarely on the bullseye of the enemy's fiery dart board.

Jude's brother James says: "My brothers, show no partiality as you hold the faith in our Lord Jesus Christ, the Lord of glory. For if a man wearing a gold ring and fine clothing comes into your assembly, and a poor man in shabby clothing also comes in, and if you pay attention to the one who wears the fine clothing and say, 'You sit here in a good place,' while you say to the poor man, 'You stand over there,' or, 'Sit down at my feet,' have you not then made distinctions among yourselves and become judges with evil thoughts?" (James 2:1-4)

James and Jude are both referring to preference given in the Church to the rich and it certainly applies and needs to be said. The commentary is not on whether there are rich and poor people or people who have more authority and those who have less; the commentary is about how we are to treat people regardless of their authority or financial realities. If we run toward them because they have or we push away from them because they have not, then we have abandoned love.

A healthy place to start asking internal questions is on the level of our motivations. Asking ourselves what our motivation is for being in a relationship is often a very revealing thing to do. If our motivation is to gain any kind of personal advantage - this could even mean simply being "seen" as caring - we have missed the heart of what it is to love others as He has loved us (John

[13] "Treasure vs. Money," sermon by Timothy Keller, The Mount; Life in the Kingdom, May 2, 1999, video, 36:20, https://www.youtube.com/watch?v=YEvuXAucbd8.

13:34-35). In fact, if our motivation is for any reason other than that person's gain in and through our discipleship of and care for them, we should take it captive and surrender it under Jesus' lordship knowing that He has pure motives that He can and wants to give us for His glory and our joy.

To be free from the tendency toward partiality requires one to work through their biases and their own personal history around which those biases have been formed. This can often be painful work because like surgery it requires us to get beneath the surface but when done correctly it is freeing work that allows for all kinds of healthy and flourishing relationships with people from all walks of life. I believe that truly honors Jesus and brings joy to those involved. [14]

REFLECTION:

Is there a situation or relationship in which you have shown partiality? If so, take a moment to ask God for forgiveness and seek His wisdom about whether you need to make restitution at all.

What biases inform your partiality and how can you shift your motivation in the future?

[14] Recommended resource: *Emotionally Healthy Spirituality,* by Peter Scazzero (Zondervan, 2017).

v. 17 - but you must remember, beloved, the predictions of the apostles of our Lord Jesus Christ.

"Beloved." There's that word again. It is a gentle reminder to us, the Church, that we are to be loved by God because of our identity as His children. It is a word that lingers with us no matter how many times we hear it or use it because it's meant to have staying power on the soul. Jude strikes at the heart in this verse by stating one way we "be loved" is to remind ourselves of the words of the apostles. In the verses that follow, he goes on to be very clear about which predictions he is presently referring to but we won't focus on that just yet. Today, let's sit inside the instruction to remember the words of the apostles.

Remembrance is at the very heart of our faith. It is Jesus our Lord who, at the last supper, gave us the gift of communion where we are to solemnly remember His broken body and shed blood as being the cornerstone of our very lives. It is also remembrance that brings us back to the center of our faith when we find ourselves wandering through days of disillusionment or doubt. To remember something is to go back in our mind's eye and visualize something to bring it into our present circumstance. To remember the things of Christ and His apostles through the eye of faith and to be able to see with that eye is a gift of grace.

Maybe today you are experiencing some real anxiety and you need to remember the Apostle Paul's words in Philippians 4:6-7. "Do not be anxious about anything, but in every situation, by prayer and petition, with thanksgiving, present your requests to God. And the peace of God, which transcends all understanding, will guard your hearts and your minds in Christ Jesus."

Or maybe you feel hopeless and need to hear the Apostle Peter's words recorded in 1 Peter 1:3-4. "Blessed be the God and Father of our Lord Jesus Christ! According to his great mercy, he has caused us to be born again to a living hope through the resurrection of Jesus Christ from the dead, to an inheritance that is imperishable, undefiled, and unfading, kept in heaven for you."

Perhaps you are in a season of doubt and need to be reminded of the surety of God's love for you. Read the Apostle John's words to you in 1 John 3:1. "See what kind of love the Father has given to us, that we should be called children of God; and so we are."

These are the words of men who saw the resurrected Christ in the flesh, given to them by the Spirit of God and delivered through them to produce joy in our lives. Our joy is married to our remembering because when we look back over our life, we can see God's faithfulness in our history as well as the history of all things. Remembering His faithfulness gives a great foundation of confidence as we look into the future because we know He will continue to be who He has always been and do what He has always done. If there is ever a time when I am frustrated or disheartened in marriage I think back to the night when I asked my wife, Jennifer, to marry me. I remember sitting at her feet with a bowl full of water and a towel as I committed to washing her feet with my life for as long as we both shall live. In the same way, when parenting my children well feels like a burden to me, I remember holding them as infants and looking into their beautiful eyes and I am quickly overcome with a sense of the blessing they are in my life.

To remember is to go back in our mind's eye to find the places of purity where purpose is clearly seen, and to bring those moments into the present. It is the same when we remember along our faith journey. We go back through the eyes of faith and place ourselves at the table reclined next to our Savior as He passes the bread and the cup, and we remember His words and His actions on the cross that brought us into an eternal common union with Him. We also go back to the shores of the Sea of Galilee when Jesus called the brothers who would become apostles as He said, "Follow Me" and we drop our nets with them and we follow Him.

We remember the words of the apostles because God gave them those words so we could remember - and in doing so, we experience Him fully.

REFLECTION:

What words of the apostles do you need to remember today?

In what ways has remembering what God has done to show you are beloved brought you renewed joy recently?

v. 18 They said to you, "In the last time there will be scoffers, following their own ungodly passions."

As a student of the scriptures, I have always found it fascinating that the apostles spoke often of the "last times". It has always seemed to me that they were convinced they were living in the last days and that Jesus' return to earth was right around the corner. I guess in an eternal sense they were right, but inside the chronology of time, as we are currently experiencing it, there have been more than 2000 years that have passed since they wrote of the last times and still we wait. The eager expectation of Christ's return was not only something the apostles were marked by; it has marked every generation of believers that has followed since. It is typical of the New Testament author's writings about the anticipation of Christ's return to be accompanied by a warning, just as Jude is doing here in our verse today.

We would do well to pay attention to these warnings and be reminded there are countless influences - both physical and spiritual - in this world trying to lead us away from the Gospel of Jesus Christ and toward a false gospel. The dominant false gospel of Jude's day was one that preached a cheap grace that gave way to license for a lifestyle of permissible sin. This led people to indulge all the desires of the flesh while believing it was what God wanted for them. Needless to say, it was a destructive false gospel that led many astray. And unfortunately, this false gospel is still alive today as well as many others.

Now, just as it was then, false gospels are built upon the deception that there is something that needs to be added to or re-interpreted in the message of Jesus (and the apostles) that we are saved by grace alone through faith alone. Some preach the false gospel that baptism or communion is a necessary requirement for salvation. Others preach a gospel that says Christ is not the only way to be reconciled to God; He is merely one of many ways. There is also a growing false gospel within the "Christian" church whereby people chase experiences that heighten emotion or intellect (or both) regardless of a lack of doctrinal purity and consistency and consider that to be faithful.

Of all the false gospels out there, I can think of none that has led more astray in recent decades than the gospel of moral therapeutic deism (MTD). That sounds fancy but here is what it teaches. Moral therapeutic deism is the belief that,

1.   *A god exists who created and ordered the world and watches over human life on earth.*
2.   *God wants people to be good, nice, and fair to each other, as taught in the Bible and by most world religions.*
3.   *The central goal of life is to be happy and to feel good about oneself.*
4.   *God does not need to be particularly involved in one's life except when God is needed to resolve a problem.*
5.   *Good people go to heaven when they die.* [15]

Unlike the heretics in Jude's day, this kind of heresy rarely comes through the mouth of a scoffer but rather through the soft lips of someone who is "enlightened" about or "in touch" with our modern culture. They are usually highly intelligent, seem incredibly caring, and are very believable. You will find this false gospel across countless self-help books that litter the best buy lists. It has flourished inside our culture's focus on our individualism teaching us that we have all we need inside us to be happy and safe. It also teaches us that what is inside us is what God wants for us so all we need to do is get in touch with our real self through right behavior and when we need God we can call on him.

However, the gospel of Jesus Christ is squarely built on the foundation of a supremely sovereign God that has placed His glory at the center of all created things and has done this because it is only His glory that can produce eternal joy for Him and for all created things. MTD subtly teaches that we are sovereign. Now it doesn't say that outright, but it trains us to subconsciously believe this by teaching us to filter all of life through the lens that we are in fact at the center of our universe.

This is not an organized religion, but it has become a normative assumption being made by many church leaders today and

---

[15] Christian Smith, *Soul Searching: The Religious and Spiritual Lives of American Teenagers* (New York, NY: Oxford University Press, 2005), 162-163.

believed by and acted upon by many fellow believers. And ultimately, many people believe their chief end is to make themselves happy through consumerism, experiences, or by any means necessary to garnish that happiness.

This is a dangerous distortion of truth. As He faithfully equips the saints in right thinking, the apostle John wrote, "Beloved, do not believe every spirit, but test the spirits to see whether they are from God, for many false prophets have gone out into the world" (1 John 4:1).

A simple and surefire test to see if something is a false gospel or not is to ask the question, "Who or what is at the center of this belief?" If at the center of the belief is not the God of Abraham, Isaac, and Jacob that incarnated Himself into flesh as Jesus of Nazareth to be born of a virgin, live sinlessly, die on a Roman cross, and rise from the dead three days later, the belief is heretical. It is a false gospel.

By grace, we stand tall and firm on the testimony of Jesus Christ as revealed to us through the Holy Bible and we stand against all false gospels knowing that the true gospel is light and life for all who will believe.

REFLECTION:

In your observation, what have false gospels cost the modern church?

How can you make sure you avoid the dangerous deception of believing a false gospel?

v. 19 – It is these who cause divisions, worldly people, devoid of the Spirit.

A division is the result of two different visions trying to occupy the same space. People divide over politics, sports teams, financial matters, cultural differences, and the list goes on and on. It doesn't matter how you try to explain division and how many details explain who's on what side and why they might be right, every division is the result of a competing vision. Husbands and wives could have different visions of what parenting should look like or how finances should be managed, bosses and employees could have different visions over what is fair and reasonable or the direction of the company, and far too often pastors and staff or laity have different visions for what the focus or the future of their local church should be. These divisions can be worked through, relationships can stay intact, and love can prevail by following Jesus' instructions in Matthew 18 as well as by using kindness and patience as a currency, but in so many cases divisions lead to separations.

The way that Jesus' followers handle divisions within the Church should be radically different than how "worldly people" who are "devoid of the Spirit" handle divisions. The kingdom of this world teaches us to talk about people, not to people. It wants us to hold grudges and walk in unforgiveness. The world would lead us to believe that people having different opinions makes them unsafe and they should be held hostage to our preferences because they don't agree with us on everything. My heart is often saddened by the reality that we have traded honoring one another for cynicism toward and distrust in one another. In the world we live in it seems to me that empathy has been replaced with criticism when we see people struggling or hurting and this is truly far from the heart of God.

As believers, we are to always work toward unity, even if that unity is to agree to disagree. The item of first importance of any division we may face has to start with the question, "Does the person I am in conflict with have the Spirit?" Jude writes of heretics who are hell-bent on deceiving the Church for selfish gain, and he says people like these should not be tolerated but instead called to repentance. If someone is trying to deceive your children and lead them astray from God, it is imperative you don't sit by idly hoping it all just works out. You have to arm yourself with God's Word and prayer to stand against the lies and the liars.

If a division arises between two believers or groups of believers we take to heart the words of the Apostle Paul when he says, "I appeal to you, brothers, by the name of our Lord Jesus Christ, that all of you agree, and that there be no divisions among you, but that you be united in the same mind and the same judgment" (1 Corinthians 1:10).

For the sake of the gospel, it is our duty as believers to strive toward a unity of mind and judgment. If we need mediators in the form of counselors or other pastors then we should pursue them. And if we need years and years of brotherly discourse to achieve unity then so be it. We should never settle for a false unity that is passive in nature, but a true unity forged in the fires of honest dialogue, trust, and the hope of Jesus Christ as the savior of all mankind. Jesus gave us the guide to how we are to handle disputes, disagreements, and any process of reconciliation in Matthew 18:15-17. "If your brother sins against you, go and tell him his fault, between you and him alone. If he listens to you, you have gained your brother. But if he does not listen, take one or two others along with you, that every charge may be established by the evidence of two or three witnesses. If he refuses to listen to them, tell it to the church. And if he refuses to listen even to the church, let him be to you as a Gentile and a tax collector." Jesus' prescriptions brought cures to soul sicknesses and wounds. His words we just read, if obeyed, can open many doors in the human heart and unleash forgiveness and honor. I invite you to seek Jesus' path of reconciliation anywhere you have a relationship that needs it.

REFLECTION:

Have you participated in a division between yourself and another believer(s)? When you look back, what would you have done differently to ensure unity between you for the sake of the gospel?

If you are currently divided with another believer, what is your course of action to prevent unnecessary separation?

DAY 28

v. 20 – But you, beloved, building yourself up on your most holy faith,

"You are saved by grace through faith, it is a gift from God, it is not of works so that no one can boast." — *Ephesians 2:8*

Faith is a gift from God. To be able to believe in Jesus Christ, and by that faith be credited His perfect righteousness, is a gift like no other. This most holy faith we have been given is signed in blood from Calvary's cross and sealed by the Holy Spirit who is working to bring about faith's full measure in our lives as He leads us toward glorification. The sweetest truth that is often hard to believe is that this redeeming faith is something completely done to us and for us and we didn't so much as lift a finger in the direction of earning it or securing it for ourselves. Accordingly, when Jude says "build yourself up on your most holy faith" he doesn't mean work harder to secure your faith. I believe he means you are to remind yourself over and over and over again of the glorious news of the Gospel of Jesus Christ because in doing so you will build up your faith on the foundations of faith.

If (when) marriage strife arises and hope for its future seems to fail, remind yourself of the fact that if the tomb of Jesus Christ is empty and death has been defeated anything is possible.

If self-hatred and or insecurities dominate your thoughts and you find it hard to rise from your bed, be reminded today that Jesus loves you so much just the way you are and that He volunteered to be beaten and murdered in your place so you would never have to taste the bitterness of death.

If your apathy has brought you to a place of total indifference in your life, relationships are hard, and you lack motivation, I have something you need to hear. The empire of Satan and his hordes of demons would seek to keep you living a life of purposeless wandering through Netflix and Instagram to pass the time are defeated and the King of all Kings has a mission for you. His mission is a glorious one whereby you get to participate in the eternal redemption of souls. There is nothing more important to define you and no one better suited to be who God created you to be than you.

Jude again uses the word 'beloved' and he does so right before He says we are to build up our faith. Something I need to hear over and over again in my life is the truth that because of Jesus Christ I am one of God's beloved children. He has given me a seat at the table in the family of God. When I was a young man and Christian, I was taught about my role in God's kingdom as a tool in the hand of God for Him to use however He saw fit. As I have matured in my life, that image is something God has gently corrected in me over time. He has revealed to me through the Gospel that I am not primarily a tool in the hand of God, but I am primarily a son in the family of God. I have found these are pretty different ways to look at who I am as a child of God. When I see myself primarily as a tool, I bend toward works-based righteousness that is very focused on what I am doing for God. This faulty thinking can easily lead me to a place where I begin to question if I am doing enough or the right kinds of things which leads me to a lot of second-guessing and doubt. However, when I trust that I am a son of God that is counted righteous not by my works but by the works of my superior older brother Jesus, the pressure to perform is off and I am able to live my life like it is a gift that has been given me for me to enjoy, which it is.

REFLECTION:

How has the enemy used relational strife, self-hatred, insecurity, or apathy as tools against your faith?

In what ways do you need to "build yourself up in the most holy faith" this week?

v. 21 – keeping yourselves in the love of God,

God loves you. He really does. All of life's struggles grow from a disbelief that God loves us and wants more for us than we could ever want for ourselves. It is this disbelief that God's enemy wants us to fall prey to and like a broken record he is constantly in our ear saying, "Did God actually say that He loves you?" And when we give his narrative a sympathetic ear, the seeds of condemnation and shame begin to sprout and choke out the joy of our salvation. I call this broken record "the whispers". Do you ever hear the whispers? I do. I hear them all the time.

This is the not-so-subtle voice of condemnation creeping around in the hallways of your soul like a bloodhound looking for any scent of flesh hiding behind closed doors. You think you are hidden from them, but the whispers are tireless, they are smart, they know you so well, and they know right where to hit you. Their names are shame, fear, and doubt and they are on a mission to take you out. I don't know exactly what they sound like to you but maybe something like this resonates:

You can't do it.
You aren't smart enough.
You are too messed up.
You're not good enough.
You've told too many lies.
You've got nothing to offer.
You're broken.
No one wants you.
You will never be free of the damage done.
You're bruised.
You can't heal.
You don't deserve love.
You need to make yourself matter and if you don't then you won't.
You aren't a good friend.
They don't really like you.
You are a letdown.
You haven't tried hard enough.
You're not safe, protect yourself.

You're what happened to you.
What happened to you is your fault because you weren't strong
enough to stop it.
They left you because you are not worth it.
You don't have any love to give.
It's all fake, no one really cares for you, they are all just faking it.
They just want something from you, and when they get it you'll
be all alone again.
You're your divorce.
You're your past sexual exploits.
You're addicted because you are an addict.
You better run.
Stay low, hide, and don't let them know who you really are.
You're going to fail.
You're a failure.
It's just a matter of time before it all falls apart.
You're too messed up to experience blessing.
You're selfish.
If fixing you was possible, you'd have done it already.
What's wrong with you?
You can't lead.
If they knew all the stuff you think about they'd never trust you.
You're not trustworthy.
You don't have what it takes.
You're a mess.
You better not tell the whole truth. Tell just enough truth to
impress but not enough to be free.
They're gone because you're not worth sticking around for.
It's all your fault.
You're going to suffer.
You're screwing your kids up.
Joy is a fine idea; you just can't have any.
Peace is not attainable in this life.
They are going to find out who you really are and when they do
it's all over.
If you were better at your job more people would be saved.
You aren't saved; you just made a religious decision.
You should worry about that.
You better get control however you can or it's all going to fall
apart.
You're the worst, why can't you be more like _____?
You're hurting everyone.

You don't hug your kids enough.
You don't love your wife well, try harder.
They died because God wants you to suffer.
You failed because you're a failure.
You're doing it again.
He doesn't love you.
If you led better, you'd be better.
Be stronger. Why are you so weak?
You aren't what you once were.
You can't keep up.
It's you, you are the problem.
You aren't a good mom.
You aren't a good spouse.
You can never live up to your parents' legacy.
You don't manage money well.
You deserve to be broke.
You're a disappointment.
You're trapped.
Give up.
Move on.
Don't trust them.
Don't trust him.
You are unhealthy because you are you.
You're lazy.
You're a liar.
If you loved God, you'd stop that.
You're small.
You're insignificant.
You talk too much.
Say something that matters for once.

All the whispers. Do any of those resonate with you? I'd imagine they do. I think of these distracting - if not totally destructive - lies as pawns in Satan's grand game of shame. All of these whispers are meant to distract you from the most powerful truth in the world - "God loves you." "For God so loved the world that He gave his only Son, that whoever believes in Him shall never perish but have eternal life" (John 3:16).

I encourage you today to go back through the list of the whispers and pick 5 of them you have commonly experienced and write them down and then write over the top of them,

"GOD LOVES YOU". God's love is stronger than any whisper, lie, deception, or distortion. His love is our anchor, and we remind ourselves we are in His love by proclaiming His love for us!

REFLECTION:

What were your five?

How does knowing that God's love is stronger than any whisper of the enemy help you overcome the lies and live in peace?

v. 21 – waiting for the mercy of our Lord Jesus Christ that leads to eternal life.

What are you waiting for?
Let's go!
Why does everyone move so slow?
Lord, where are you?
We need to get it together and get things done!
Why wait until tomorrow to do what can be done today?

I don't know about you, but waiting is averse to my personality due in large part to the culture of the day. We like fast, we want things when we want them, and we don't want to wait to get them. So often, though, we miss out on the beauty of the process the Lord has us in because we are in such a hurry to get to the destination we believe we deserve.

Thankfully, the Lord is patient with us. "The Lord is not slow to fulfill his promise as some count slowness, but is patient toward you, not wishing that any should perish, but that all should reach repentance" (2 Peter 3:9).

He is taking His time as He is reconciling all things unto Himself (2 Corinthians 5:19). He knows what we don't know, and He can see what we can't fathom (Isaiah 55:8-9). How many prayers have you prayed in your life that you are now thankful God didn't answer or that He answered differently than you thought He should at the time? I believe one of the reasons the Lord has placed patience at the center of living a full life is because He wants us to want Him and waiting for Him reminds us we aren't Him and we need Him. It is God's grace toward us that He would make us wait, and it is His mercy on us to be present with us in the waiting.

In his masterpiece A Long Obedience in the Same Direction, Eugene Peterson writes, "A person has to get fed up with the ways of the world before he, before she, acquires an appetite for the world of grace." [16]

---

[16] Eugene H. Peterson, *A Long Obedience in the Same Direction: Discipleship in an Instant Society* (Westmont, IL: InterVarsity Press, 2012), 25.

How sweet it is to tire of this dying world while we long for the fullness of Jesus' mercy to be made known to us in eternity. You can trust the Father today.

You can trust that He has you firmly in His grip and He is working out your glorification according to His divine plan.
You can trust that He is not done with you yet but that He will finish what He has started.
You can trust that He is merciful and good, that His love is steadfast and unfailing.
You can trust that He will never leave you, never forsake you.
You can trust that you may walk through the valley of the shadow of death, and He will make you lie down in green pastures as He restores your soul.
You can trust that He is not angry with you, but He is, in fact, in love with you.

Is your soul restless? Are you filled with tension and anxiety that bubbles just beneath the surface of your life? Are you dismayed with your circumstances or frustrated by what seems like a lack of response from the Lord? I have been there as well, so let me encourage you to slow down, take some time off, step away from trying to make things happen for yourself, and be alone with the Lord. There is no replacement that can produce more peace for the believer than long uninterrupted times spent alone with the Lord through prayer and the reading of His Word. It is in the places of calm and quiet that the soul connects to the patience of eternity and is reminded God is speaking His goodness into every corner of our lives. Rest today in His Word as you plan to spend time with Him.

"God is our refuge and strength, a very present help in trouble. Therefore, we will not fear though the earth gives way, though the mountains be moved into the heart of the sea, The LORD of hosts is with us; the God of Jacob is our fortress. He makes wars cease to the end of the earth; he breaks the bow and shatters the spear; he burns the chariots with fire. Be still, and know that I am God. I will be exalted among the nations, I will be exalted in the earth!" (Psalm 46:1-3,7,9-10).

REFLECTION:

What makes waiting hard for you?

What are you waiting for God to do? Write it down and spend a few minutes praying about it right now.

v. 22-23 – And have mercy on those who doubt; save others by snatching them out of the fire; to others show mercy with fear,

There is nothing more inherent to being a Christ-follower than the desire to see others saved by grace through faith. When we are saved and rescued by Jesus we are immediately put on the rescue team to help others get rescued as well (2 Corinthians 5:18-19). There is nothing that produces more joy in our lives and in the kingdom than when one person turns away from sin and death and toward life through repentance.

"There will be more joy in heaven over one sinner who repents than over ninety-nine righteous persons who need no repentance." – *Jesus (Luke 15:7)*

I have met many believers through the years who struggle with finding and walking in their purpose. Most of the time this struggle is experienced because people believe that their purpose terminates on their internal sense of fulfillment. It does not. When happiness and fulfillment are experienced, they are a welcomed byproduct of walking as someone who has been given purpose but they are not the point for which God gives us purpose. Our earthly purpose as Jesus-followers is to make disciples. We are to lead other people to the truth of Jesus Christ and help them walk in loving union with Him. That's it. We can do this as moms, dads, co-workers, bosses, pastors, small group leaders, missionaries, plumbers, coaches, or nurses. Where we make disciples is secondary to being committed to making disciples.

Further, we often overcomplicate the simplicity of the truth of the Good News. The truth is that saved people spend eternity in heaven filled with joy, hope, peace, and purpose without end or contest because of what Christ did on the cross, and people who are not saved spend eternity in hell apart from Christ, being filled with hate, selfishness, bitterness, and hopelessness. It really is that clear, and we should be willing to do anything short of sin to see people receive God's love and forgiveness unto salvation.

The way I read Jude's words is to "do whatever you have to and whatever you can to see people turn to Jesus." There is always much debate about the most effective ways to evangelize the lost, and admittedly there are some ways that are simply better than others. But the bottom line is we have been trusted with the most important words in the world:

"That is, in Christ God was reconciling the world to himself, not counting their trespasses against them, and entrusting to us the message of reconciliation" (2 Corinthians 5:19).

"For God so loved the world, that He gave His only begotten Son, that whoever believes in Him shall not perish, but have eternal life. "For God did not send the Son into the world to judge the world, but that the world might be saved through Him. "He who believes in Him is not judged; he who does not believe has been judged already, because he has not believed in the name of the only begotten Son of God" (John 3:16-18).

So I ask you today, who is it that God has placed in your life that has not placed their faith in Jesus Christ for salvation? Pray for them and ask God to open a door for you to share with them what He has done for them through Jesus. Then, send them a text right now and invite them to coffee, a meal, or a conversation and let's see what God does.

We can rest assured that as deeply as we want them to come to repentance God's love and desire for them runs far deeper. He is at work. Let's join Him in it!

REFLECTION:

For whom are you praying for their salvation?

In what ways have you confused or convoluted the simple, but powerful message of the gospel?

v. 23 – hating even the garment defiled by the flesh.

If you are a parent or can imagine being one – How would you feel if every day all day someone was following your child around telling them lies and trying to destroy all that you know they are capable of and taking away from them any possibility of being happy? You'd hate that, right? Of course, you would. Well, on a very small level, that gives us a small glimpse into how God feels about sin. Saying He's not a fan of sin's effects on His children would be a pretty dramatic understatement. Saying He hates it is more accurate - and even that is a feeble attempt at expressing it rooted in a futile language. If you believe the Bible, then it is clear sin is not a problem, sin is the problem.

"What is sin" is an important question to ask because every human I have ever met, myself the chief among them, thinks that sin is an "issue," or at its most severe, it is a "struggle." The cognitive human effort that seeks to pioneer a sense of freedom has led us down a path from which, apart from the divine intervening work of the Spirit of God, we can't return from. This effort has sought to redefine the parameters of human responsibility and God's sovereignty. And at its very core, it is an attack on the foundation of what it means to be human. You see, if you do not have a right, concise, and biblically-whole definition of what sin really is, then it is impossible to treasure the grace that shines against the backdrop of depravity.

Is it possible that we have traded beauty for ashes by minimizing what sin really is? Is it possible that we are so good at justifying sin that we have created a definition of sin that works for us but falls desperately short of biblically faithful? Sin is not just something we do or something we have done, and it is not just a mistake we made or an error in thinking or speech. There's more gravity to it than that. It goes well beyond our limited constructs of cultural morality and even presses in deeper beyond the right and wrongs of the law. Sin is not some well-meaning attempt that failed or an activity that happens outside the body and is somehow separate from the intentions inside the human soul.

Sin is a state of being. It is a powerful force coded into our DNA. It is alive, it is aggressive, it is deceptive, and it is impossible to cure in and of our own efforts. It is, in a very practical sense, a deep rejection of God's ultimate good and God's glorious rule. In essence, sin is the non-supremacy of God who was made manifest in the person of Jesus Christ. So it is fair and right to say that, in essence, sin is the non-supremacy of Christ.

Sin, therefore, can be rightly defined as any feeling, thought, speech, or action that comes from a heart that does not treasure Christ over all things. It is a heart that gives preference to anything over God......ever.

So what is sin? Dr. John Piper offers us this definition:

Sin is the glory of God not honored.
The holiness of God not reverenced.
The greatness of God not admired.
The power of God not praised.
The truth of God not sought.
The wisdom of God not esteemed.
The beauty of God not treasured.
The goodness of God not savored.
The promises of God not believed.
The commandments of God not obeyed.
The justice of God not respected.
The wrath of God not feared.
The grace of God not cherished.
The presence of God not prized.
The person of God not loved. [17]

I would add to Dr. Piper's very thorough definition that sin is also the gospel of God not trusted.

That's what sin is and God has such disdain for it that He, "shows his love for us in that while we were still sinners, Christ died for us" (Romans 5:8). While we are clothed in the very thing God hates, instead of abandoning us to our filth, He volunteers Himself to become the very thing He hates on the cross so that we could forever be the thing that His Father loves.

---

[17] John Piper, "Sin Prefers Anything to God," *Desiring God,* April 8, 2015, https://www.desiringgod.org/interviews/sin-prefers-anything-to-god.

It's simply mind-numbing, isn't it? If we loved God the way He loves us then we would hate sin the way that He hates sin.

One day we will see everything as He sees it – including sin. Until then, we hold tight to His mercy.

REFLECTION:

What misperceptions of sin have you had in the past and how did they distort your view of yourself?

v. 24 – Now to him who is able to keep you from stumbling and to present you blameless before the presence of his glory with great joy.

Have you ever been blamed for something you didn't do? How did you handle it? I bet you responded with grace and compassion like you always do. Me too! Every. Time...

Have you ever been blamed for something you actually did? How did you respond to it? Did you immediately lay down your arms and surrender in repentance? Did you jump at the mercy of those who you wronged, admitting all fault? Yeah. Again, me too...

The point is, we don't like being blamed for things. Hating blame, dodging blame, and blame-shifting are tactics as old as sin, literally. When God confronts Adam in the garden after he had eaten of the forbidden tree and shame set in through nakedness, God asks, "'Who told you that you were naked? Have you eaten of the tree of which I commanded you not to eat?' The man said, 'The woman whom you gave to be with me, she gave me fruit of the tree, and I ate.' Then the LORD God said to the woman, 'What is this that you have done?' The woman said, 'The serpent deceived me, and I ate'" (Genesis 3:11-13).

Adam nor eve was interested in taking the blame for what they had done. This is just another reason why what Christ has done for us on the cross is so remarkable. He took the blame for our sin so we could have credit for His righteousness. Let's read that again:

Jesus took the blame for our sin so we could have credit for his righteousness.

Don't just breeze right past that. Let me ask you this while you are sitting there with your cup of coffee: Do you have any idea what Jesus has done for you? Really?

I am not talking about your run-of-the-mill "God loves you so he sent Jesus to die for you" Instagram post at Easter time. I am talking about the real thing. I am talking about the blood-soaked atrocity of the cross of Calvary. I am talking about the creation-splitting, earthquake-making, dead-people-getting-up-out-of-the-grave-and-walking-around-the-city event that happened 2000 years ago. I am talking about the Holy God of all perfection having every ounce of His perfection honored, upheld, and satisfied through volunteering Himself to be murdered. For us.

I am talking about credit and blame. I am talking about the person who has had all the credit for every good thing ever done. Every good name ever given, every good deed ever accomplished, and every flower that blooms or bird that sings or star that radiates or every wave that crashes declaring God's infinite glory is rightfully His claim. The Son has since forever past received credit for the creation and operation of all things. All of them.

He is the one who deserves the credit and, He has been getting the credit since forever.

He took all the blame. All of it. He took the blame. The blame for what, you ask. Well, everything.

Whose blame, you ask. Well, the blame of everyone who will believe. Your blame and my blame, all of it for all of us who are His beloved. Dang, He is good.

REFLECTION:

When was the last time you blamed someone or something else for your sin?

Write down any sin God wants you to acknowledge and repent of today along with a prayer of gratitude that He took it all upon Himself.

v. 25 – to the only God, our Savior, through Jesus Christ our Lord,

As His people wander the wilderness, God leads Moses to the top of Mt. Sinai and reveals to him the very fabric of the universe in the first commandment, "'I am the Lord your God, who brought you out of the land of Egypt, out of the house of slavery. You shall have no other gods before me'" (Exodus 20:1-3).

And then again, He gifts the knowledge of Himself as the cornerstone on which all life is to be understood through prayer. "Hear, O Israel: The Lord our God, the Lord is one. You shall love the Lord your God with all your heart and with all your soul and with all of your might" (Deuteronomy 6:4-5).

To the prophet Isaiah, He said, "For I am God, and there is none else; I am God, and there is none like me"(Isaiah 46:9).

And in the New Testament, the one and only true God gifts Himself not only in promise but in the flesh. "And this is life eternal, that they might know the only true God, and Jesus Christ, whom you have sent" (John 17:3). "For there is one God, and one mediator between God and men, the man Christ Jesus" (1 Timothy 2:5).

The exclusivity of God being God is the most central and important doctrinal tenet which must be accepted and believed in order for any of the rest of the Gospel of God to be understood. This truth is known as monotheism. Christianity is not the only monotheistic religion in the world. Judaism and Islam are both monotheistic as well, but Christianity is distinct because it is Trinitarian, meaning we believe God the Father, God the Son, and God the Holy Spirit are three in one. And we embrace this as the foundation stone of our faith that the one God who created our universe is eternal. We believe He is all-knowing, all-present, and all-powerful. And while it is supremely important to believe in the one, true living trinitarian God of the Bible, that belief alone does not lead to salvation. It is easy to believe philosophically there is one creator God or to make a logical defense of His existence. The Bible tells us even the demons believe (James 2:19). So yes, monotheism is needed, beautiful, fundamental, and to be rejoiced in, but it is not enough to set us free from the wage of sin.

Jesus, monotheism in the flesh, tells us, "I am the way, the truth, and the life, no one comes to the Father except through me" (John 14:6).

Jesus is the God-man. He is the one true living God and He came to earth to save us from our sins. Salvation comes to those who believe in the truth that Jesus is God and He came as a man who lived a perfect life and then died a sacrificial death on the cross as the penalty for the sins of all those who would believe, but He did not stay dead; He rose again three days later. We don't only believe in this truth as a concept, we believe in true events that happened to a real person in Israel more than 2000 years ago.

Paul says if we "confess with our mouths that Jesus is Lord and believe in our hearts that God raised him from the dead then we shall be saved" (Romans 10:9). Paul doesn't say we might be saved or God would consider saving us if we confess and believe; he assures us we shall be saved. What Jesus has done could only be done by God Himself, and it is upon this miracle - and the One and only God who could do this miracle - we stake our very eternities through faith.

REFLECTION:

If you were going to explain the means by which we are saved to a non-believer, what would you say?

v. 25 - be glory,

Glory means praise, honor, or distinction extended. [18] God's glory is His holiness put on display for all created things to see. His glory is the measure of His significance, which is immeasurable. We are created for His glory. We are to give Him glory. We are saved for His glory. We are going to share in His glory for all eternity. The amount of content which could be written about God's glory is absolutely endless because of its width, depth, and power. God's glory is God's primary motivation for doing anything He does. And He is always working to display and preserve His beauty, perfection, and infinite greatness.

In a similar manner to gravity, God's glory is all around us and it's central to our lives and to the very fabric of our universe. To say God is glorious is to say there is an absolute reality around which all human love, wonder, inspiration, praise, and affection are centered. We know of this reality deep in our bones, and yet, it is what we spend our time and energy looking for in this lifetime. We want to be filled with His glory and consumed by it because it is the only real thing in the world that can finally satisfy the deep longing of our souls.

Often, when we talk of God's glory we speak of it as if it is some far-off land we are waiting to enjoy or like it is a mysterious spirit floating just above the ceiling, and if we sing loud enough or preach long enough maybe it will fall on us. It is neither. Hebrews 1:3 says that "He (Jesus) is the radiance of the glory of God and the exact imprint of his nature" (emphasis mine). We do not have to go any further than the person of Jesus to see, savor, and be enthralled by and with God's infinite glory. Jesus is God's glory on perfect display for us to know Him by. Jesus isn't hiding God's glory from us. In fact, He prayed in John 17:24 that "they may be with me where I am, to see my glory."

Jesus prayed for you! How cool is that? And when He did, He asked God for you and me to be able to see His glory. I believe this is a prayer request God has answered by giving us eyes of faith by which we see Jesus as the King of all Kings. I also

---

[18] *Merriam-Webster*, s.v. "glory," accessed March 2, 2022, https://www.merriam-webster.com/dictionary/glory.

believe Jesus' prayer request is still being answered as we inch closer and closer to the day when we live in the new heavenly city where "the glory of God gives it light and its lamp is the Lamb" (Revelation 21:23).

The fact that God's primary motivation is His glory is the best news in the world. There is no one I have found that has written more eloquently or accurately about the magnificence and joy which is God's glory than Jonathan Edwards. Here are some of his words: "God is the highest good of the reasonable creature. The enjoyment of him is our proper; and is the only happiness with which our souls can be satisfied. To go to heaven, fully to enjoy God, is infinitely better than the most pleasant accommodations here. Better than fathers and mothers, husbands, wives, or children, or the company of any, or all earthly friends. These are but shadows; but the enjoyment of God is the substance. These are but scattered beams; but God is the sun. These are but streams; but God is the fountain. These are but drops, but God is the ocean. God's purpose for my life was that I have a passion for God's glory and that I have a passion for my joy in that glory, and that these two are one passion. Grace is but glory begun, and glory is but grace perfected. He who has Christ has all he needs and needs no more." [19]

To trust in Jesus is to be wrapped up in the glory of God. It is to have found a diamond of endless depth and beauty and to have the ability to stare into it endlessly, always seeing more beauty, worth, and significance.

As we go about our lives today, and for all of our days, may we join with God in making His glory central to all our decisions, actions, and efforts. And by doing so, may we experience the unending joy which can only be produced by His infinite Glory at work in our finite lives.

---

[19] Jonathan Edwards, *The Works of Jonathan Edwards, Vol. 17: Sermons and Discourses, 1730-1733,* accessed March 2, 2022, https://www.goodreads.com/quotes/99178-god-is-the-highest-good-of-the-reasonable-creature-the.

REFLECTION:

In what ways have you experienced God's glory in the last few weeks?

How can you make God's glory known today?

v. 25 - majesty,

There is no one like Him, there is no God but Him.

He was and is and is to come, He reigns on high over all things visible and invisible.

His ways are higher, His thoughts are wiser, His beauty is matchless, and His sovereignty is sure.

He is everywhere, ahead of everything, and behind everything. There is nothing that happens that does not first pass through His hands.

He holds the endless galaxies in His hands and knows the stars by the names He has given each one.

Before the beginning, He set at the foundation of the world a cross and made atonement for all sins of His children so they could be redeemed by His mercy and secured for His glory.

Every whisper of wind and calamity of storm declares His might. Every rolling wave and soaring eagle give way to His presence. Every child's tear and every mother's embrace arrive by the merciful touch of God.

To be near Him is to be alive, to be His is to be immortal. He is unending beyond time, never-changing in character nor intention, incomprehensible in mercy, and more available to His children than gravity is to the earth.

He did not begin when the beginning began but He began the beginning; He did not start when start started, He started start. At a word He brought forth day and night, land and sea, and all things that crawl, swim, and fly. He leaned in and breathed the life of an eternal soul into His prized creation, and up from the dirt came His image, staring back at Him, reflecting Him to His creation, just as the moon reflects the sun.

He is the Lord God of Israel, the Lion of Judah, the righteous one of the remnant, the Prince of Peace, the King of all Kings, the firstborn among the dead, the resurrected Christ, the Messiah, and the Lamb that was slain before the foundations of the world.

He is the joy that comes in the morning. He is the eternity that has been set in the hearts of man and the true north which guides us home. He has ten thousand times ten thousand angels declaring His glory and angels of fire flying around His throne declaring His nature singing, "Holy, Holy, Holy is the Lord God almighty."

His love never fails and His hope endures forever. It is with gladness He does all things, and there is nothing that runs deeper through the veins of creation than His grace. His purpose is undeniable and His mission is unwavering.

It is in Him, through Him, for Him, by Him, and to Him that all things that have been created were created. He can't be stopped, won't be forgotten, and shall never be moved nor forsaken.

His name is above every name on earth and in heaven, and He has set a feast for his family that will forever be their joy. He has no fear, He has no shame, He is guilty of nothing, and He will always finish what He starts. He is all-knowing, all-powerful, all-loving, and good. He is tenacious in dispensing His grace, He is ferocious in battle, undefeated, irrevocable, and supreme in all His ways.

He is majesty.

REFLECTION:

Pick three attributes from the list above and look up verses to support these statements.

How do the attributes you selected depict His majesty and what do they mean to your heart?

v. 25 - dominion,

Dominion is not a word that we are accustomed to referring to because it usually has a negative connotation when referring to someone's rule and reign over others. It is also used aside when drawing lines of governance for nations. It technically means "the territory of a sovereign." [20]

To say that Christ has dominion is to say everything is His territory. This is fitting because all things do belong to Him and are under His sovereign control. This is nothing clearer than when God speaks through the prophet Isaiah saying, "Heaven is my throne, and the earth is my footstool" (Isaiah 66:1).

Jesus the Christ, who sits on the throne of grace at the right hand of the Father, uses the earth as a footstool. This is how the Bible communicates His total dominion. There is nothing that happens that does not first pass through the hands of Christ, and in that truth we find great confidence as His people. But in order to really get our head around the realities of His dominion, we have to go back to the beginning.

When God created Adam, He gave him dominion over all created things. "Then God said, 'Let us make man in our image, after our likeness. And let them have dominion over the fish of the sea and over the birds of the heavens and over the livestock and over all the earth and over every creeping thing that creeps on the earth.' So God created man in his own image, in the image of God he created him, male and female he created them. And God blessed them. And God said to them, 'Be fruitful and multiply and fill the earth and subdue it and have dominion over the fish of the sea and over the birds of the heavens and over every living thing that moves on the earth'" (Genesis 1:26-28).

God gave Adam a great responsibility and created him with everything he needed in order to accomplish such a trusted task. This incredible gift of dominion was God's gift to all of mankind.

[20] *Encyclopedia Online*, s.v. "dominion," last modified May 23, 2018, https://www.encyclopedia.com/social-sciences-and-law/political-science-and-government/political-science-terms-and-concepts/dominion.

Inside this gift is the mandate to flourish and bring flourishing forth. We were to cultivate an environment whereby all created things walk in accordance with their God-given purpose. And in doing so, creation reflects back to God His infinite worth - primarily through the means of our enjoyment of the things He placed under our rule or dominion.

But, as we well know, Adam screwed it up royally. Instead of flourishing with dominion, Adam chose to fall and surrender his dominion to God's enemy, Satan, and by doing so bring death to creation.

Paul helps us understand the generational impact of Adam's surrender of dominion in Romans 5:13-14. "Death reigned from Adam to Moses, even over those who had not sinned according to the likeness of the transgression of Adam, who is a type of Him who was to come."

So instead of passing on a lineage of dominion whereby all things flourish, Adam passed on a lineage of death whereby all things wander around looking for their purpose that he gave away. This is known as federalism. Federalism simply has to do with the idea of representation. It is when one person or group of people acts on behalf of another or others. Our government in America is a federalism, which means we elect people to act on our behalf. God created Adam and appointed him to act on our behalf, but he did not do a good job, and because he dropped the ball in such a severe manner his sin was written on the hearts of all men for all time. Because he sinned, all have sinned. Some would argue the "law" as revealed to Moses created sin, but it certainly did not. Paul clearly articulates in Romans 5 that the law made clear what was already known, which is that all men are sinners.

The good news is But. God. "But God shows his love for us in this that while we were still sinners, Christ died for us" (Romans 5:8). See, God didn't abandon humanity; instead He invaded it. Adam was not the only one appointed with federal headship, Christ has it as well. By faith, we come out from under the federal rule of Adam to live under the federal rule of Christ. In Paul's letter to the Corinthians, he makes this clear. "For as by a man came death, by a man has come also the resurrection of the dead. For as in Adam all die, so also in Christ shall all be made alive" (1 Corinthians 15:21-22).

Christ is our representative. He elected Himself to be so. And as He hang on the cross, He bore the punishment for Adam's sin as well as mine and yours so we could wear His perfect robe of righteousness. He became death so we could have life. This cosmic move of mercy restores us into our rightful place of dominion so we can now enjoy God's creation and exercise dominion over it, living out the very purpose for which God created us.

REFLECTION:

What areas of your life do you still struggle to give God dominion?

v. 25 - authority,

To say Christ is the authority over all things is to say He gets the last word. And indeed, He does. This is, on the most fundamental level, what it means to be Lord; it means you have the authority.

In Matthew 28, when Jesus gifts all those who will ever become His disciples the great commission, He says, "All authority on heaven and earth has been given to me" (Matthew 28:19). To recognize Jesus as our authority is to recognize Him for who He is.

There have been those through the Church ages who have taught that Jesus as Savior and Jesus as Lord are two different things. They would lead us to believe it is possible to be "saved" but not be submitted under Jesus' authority as a way of life. I just can't get there biblically. Of course, people struggle, are selfish, and are a work in progress of sanctification, but you can struggle under Jesus' lordship and He will be closer than a brother to you in that struggle; but it's altogether different than struggling against Jesus' lordship.

To be surrendered to the lordship of Jesus Christ is to be surrendered to His authority in all things. It is to say "I willfully want to spend my life telling my pride no, giving of all that I have for His agenda, loving others at great cost to myself, forgiving fast and seeking forgiveness from others faster, repenting always, and being wholly aware of my complete dependence on His grace for all things. I want what He wants and when I don't, I will deny myself and go with Him anyway. I believe He has earned the right for my love and devotion because of who He is and what He has done for me which I do not deserve. I do all these things by faith because by faith I believe what He has planned for me is better than anything I could've planned for myself."

The joy of following Jesus as Lord is exactly what it sounds like, it is choosing to follow Jesus' example and teaching over anything else. Whether it be cultural norms, our feelings, the powers that be, or the whispers of our past which seek to make themselves lord over us, we have a higher authority in Christ and we do what He says because we are who He says!

Our brother and martyr of the faith, Dietrich Bonhoeffer, says it like this: "Discipleship never consists in this or that specific action: it is always a decision, either for or against Jesus Christ... Christ speaks to us exactly as he spoke to them (1st-century disciples). It was not as though they first recognized him as the Christ and then received his command. They believed his Word and command and recognized him as the Christ--in that order." [21] It is God's design and desire that we are united in heart, soul, mind, and strength in submission to His authority. Our invitation today, as it is every day, is to align all of who we are with all of what His Word tells us – be true to who He is and what He desires. And as we align our lives under His command, we begin to experience the full life He offers us (John 10:10). Living the full life offered by Jesus means that we live aware of His presence in all the ordinariness of life. And as we sense and experience His presence, ordinary things can be enjoyed as supernatural gifts.

REFLECTION:

Is Jesus Lord and Savior over your entire life?

Are there any areas where you are living willfully not under His authority?

---

[21] Dietrich Bonhoeffer, *The Cost of Discipleship* (New York: Macmillan, 1966), 250.

v. 25 - before all time and now and forever.

We have these deep yearnings inside us which never seem to go away. We want to belong. We want to have significance. We want to experience justice. We want unity. We want peace. We want people, communication, and something beyond us which explains to us where our deepest longings comes from and how they can be satisfied. We want our lives to mean something. What everyone on the planet is looking for, whether they are aware of it or not, is God. What, or better yet, who we want is the trinitarian God of the Bible. Our deepest needs, which are seemingly never satisfied through our own personal pursuits, point us to the relationship which we were originally created to enjoy through a loving union with God.

The trinity has always been since the beginning of time, and it always will be. God's eternal experience in relationship to Himself has and will always be shalom or universal flourishing. The Father, the Son who is Jesus, and the Holy Spirit never disagree and they never shame each other or one-up each other. The godhead's experience is one of mutual, voluntary submission in all things all the time. God has always had a perfect relationship in, and with Himself. The trinity is completely self-sufficient and has need of nothing. God did not create man out of a need to be worshipped or any other kind of need; He created man out of His nature to love. He created us so we could enjoy Him through a loving union with Him in the same way He has always enjoyed Himself.

The consistent rhythm of Father, Son, and Spirit is that the Father glorifies the Son who glorifies the Spirit who glorifies the Father who glorifies the Son. It is an unbroken circle of love that runs eternally in a straight line that has no beginning or end.

The offer of salvation is an offer to be reunited in heart, soul, mind, and strength with the undivided God who is three in one. In the trinity, we see a humbling picture of God's relationship with Himself which is the portrait of what real life is supposed to be like. How gracious it is of God to show us openly what He could have easily kept a secret! We don't just see our beginning or original purpose through the trinity; we see our end as well.

When Jesus was asked by a Jewish scribe, "What is the greatest commandment?", which is like ultimately asking Him, "What is the most important thing in the world?", Jesus responded with, "The most important is, 'Hear, O Israel: The Lord our God, the Lord is one. And you shall love the Lord your God with all your heart and with all your soul and with all your mind and with all your strength" (Mark 12:29-30).

If we are not careful, we could jump right to what we believe is our part, which is to love God with all our heart, soul, mind, and strength, and miss the point of His love completely. The point is not to try harder to love God or categorically get your life in order through a deeper devotion to God. The point is "The Lord our God, The Lord is one" (Deuteronomy 6:4). He is undivided and undefeated. The most important thing in the world is that we catch a vision of the one true living God. When we see Him for who He is, Father, Son, and Spirit, we will respond to Him in worship. And from a place of humble response, our love for Him will grow and our devotion to Him will mature.

He was, as Jude says, before all time and He will be now and forever. His offer to us is to look upon Him, to get lost in awe as we consider His wonder, and to believe in His name and rejoice in His nature. He has invited us to be quiet before Him and listen as He sings over us. He has called us by His name and placed us in Christ so we have access to His throne room of grace where we go boldly asking, seeking, and knocking in confidence that our Father, our brother, and our friend is listening.

REFLECTION:

What things have you substituted as hollow alternatives to God's rightful place in your life?

In what ways has your love and devotion to God grown recently?

v. 25 - Amen.

Will you pray with me?

Father, thank You for my friend who has spent the last 40 days studying the book of Jude with me. I pray You would bless them, keep them, and cause Your face to shine upon them so Your ways would be known in their life, in their family, and to the world through them.

Holy Spirit, I ask you to fill their mind with the peace of the Kingdom of God, their soul with Your presence, their heart with Your love, and their body with Your strength so Your joy would be found complete in their life as they follow You and help others to do the same.

Jesus, I pray you would be their highest treasure and you would truly be before all things in their life as You continue to reveal to them the heights, widths, and depths to which You have gone in order for them to be a part of Your family forever. Please show them You are the way in any area of life where they are having a hard time finding their way. Show them You are the truth if there is anywhere they believe or are being tempted to believe a lie and that You are the experience of true life. I pray their best and fullest days of life are ahead of them in Your precious and powerful name!

Amen.

Friend, thank you for inviting me into your time with the Lord. I have truly been honored to be a part of your journey to deepening your relationship with Him.

If I can pray for you or you just want to say hi, please email me at **ryan.britt@coe22.com**. I'd love to hear from you!

ACKNOWLEDGMENTS

Thank you to Pastor Joby Martin and the elders of our church for giving me the chance to encourage our church through this devotional.

Thank you to the crazy talented team of men and women I serve alongside on staff at our church, you are all truly amazing!

Thank you to my wife Jennifer for everything; who or where would I be without you? God only knows.

Finally, thank you to my dad. You taught me to love God and His Word, which is the greatest of all gifts!

ABOUT THE AUTHOR

Ryan Britt is husband to Jennifer and dad to Anna Kathryn
and Abigail. He serves as the Executive Pastor of Ministries at
The Church of Eleven22 in Jacksonville, Florida.

BIBLIOGRAPHY

Bonhoeffer, Dietrich. *The Cost of Discipleship*. New York: Macmillan, 1966.

Chan, Francis. *Erasing Hell: What God Said About Eternity, and the Things We've Made Up*. Colorado Springs: David C. Cook, 2011.

Edwards, Jonathan. *The Works of Jonathan Edwards, Vol. 17: Sermons and Discourses, 1730-1733*. Accessed March 2, 2022. https://www.goodreads.com/quotes/99178-god-is-the-highest-good-of-the-reasonable-creature-the.

Evans, Tony. *Praying Through the Names of God*. Eugene: Harvest House Publishers, 2014.

Graham, Billy. *Graham 2in1 - Angels: God's Secret Angels / Peace with God*. Nashville: Thomas Nelson, 2009.

Keller, Timothy. "Treasure vs. Money." YouTube. May 2, 1999. https://www.youtube.com/watch?v=YEvuXAucbd8.

Peterson, Eugene H. *A Long Obedience in the Same Direction: Discipleship in an Instant Society*. Westmont: InterVarsity Press, 2012.

Piper, John. "Contend for the Faith." *Desiring God*. November 25, 1984. https://www.desiringgod.org/messages/contend-for-the-faith.

----------, "Sin Prefers Anything to God." *Desiring God*. April 8, 2015. https://www.desiringgod.org/interviews/sin-prefers-anything-to-god.

Graham Ryken, Philip. *Exodus: Saved for God's Glory*. Wheaton, IL: Crossway Books, 2015.

Smith, Christian. *Soul Searching: The Religious and Spiritual Lives of American Teenagers*. New York: Oxford University Press, 2005.

Spurgeon, Charles Haddon. *All of Grace: An Earnest Word with Those who are Seeking Salvation by the Lord Jesus Christ*. United Kingdom: Passmore and Alabaster, 1897.

Swindoll, Chuck. "Jude." *Insight for Living Ministries*. Accessed March 2, 2022. https://insight.org/resources/bible/the-general-epistles/jude.